Managing in the Service Economy

Instructor's Handbook

JAMES L. HESKETT

Harvard Business School

Harvard Business School Press, Boston 02163

ISBN 0-87584-143-0

TABLE OF CONTENTS

MANAGING IN THE SERVICE ECONOMY
INSTRUCTOR'S HANDBOOK

This handbook suggests ways in which the book, Managing in the Service Economy, can be used for instruction. Managing in the Service Economy analyzes and appraises various types of service businesses and highlights those aspects of service business that differ most greatly from manufacturing firms. At the same time, the book provides a comprehensive framework, comprising basic and integrative elements of a "strategic service vision" for the study of service business problems. The book fulfills a need for background material that provides multifunctional coverage for service management courses.

Managing in the Service Economy can supplement lectures, readings, and cases in courses dealing with services marketing, the management of service operations, or more generally, service firm management. The book has been used successfully in executive programs as well as in longer, more formal academic courses, particularly those offered to students with some background in functional aspects of business.

PLAN OF THE HANDBOOK

This handbook is designed to assist in the development of course outlines that make use of the book. First, there is a set of questions for class discussion based on reading assignments in the book; these questions encourage students to think beyond the material they have read rather than parrot it. They make reference to the introduction and appendices of the book as well as to the chapters, reflecting the importance of both the head and end notes for discussion purposes.

The handbook's next section suggests corollary materials, which include a number of readings and more than a hundred cases and other resources, that have been used successfully in connection with the text material.

Finally, a number of outlines for longer formal academic courses in services management, services marketing, and the management of service operations are presented, along with those for a series of shorter executive seminars. Such seminars include both general services management courses and a series of seminars oriented to each of several types of service industries, reflecting the growing body of teaching material in such areas as banking, food and lodging, communications and information, financial, retailing, transportation, and professional services. For ideas for organizing courses and sequencing--particularly case materials--I am indebted to those with whom I have taught at the Harvard Business School, especially W. Earl Sasser, Jr., the late D. Daryl Wyckoff, David H. Maister, and Christopher H. Lovelock.

Most of the material referenced here is used in my own courses; I have found it among the most enjoyable of all I have taught, of great natural interest to students who become, in turn, highly motivated by it. I hope that your experiences are the same.

SUGGESTED ASSIGNMENT QUESTIONS FOR DISCUSSION

Introduction

1. What criteria other than that cited on p. 2, "the intangibility of what is being bought," might be used to delineate industries in the service sector?

2. Which industries would or would not fit under each of the alternate criteria you proposed in question 1?

3. What are basic differences between the "game between persons" and the "game against fabricated nature" mentioned on p. 2?

4. Do you agree with the quote attributed to Marvin Harris on p. 2 that "there is no conceivable realm of profitable employment whose expansion can make up for even modest productivity gains among the nation's sixty million service-and-information workers"? Why?

5. When did service-producing jobs as a proportion of the total shown in Figure A-1, p. 180, begin to accelerate most rapidly? What reasons could you advance for this?

6. Given the outstanding performance of at least the stocks included in the Cambridge Service Index, shown in Figure A-2, p. 181, how do you explain the fact that the Dow Jones Industrial Index has been the best-known stock index throughout the twentieth century?

7. Which of the countries listed in Table A-3, p. 184, did you least expect to see listed there? Why?

8. Did the data in Table A-1, p. 182, confirm your preconceptions about the growth of federal government? Why?

9. Based on data presented in Appendix B, do you agree with the comment of one U.S. Department of Labor economist that "a case can be made based on job figures that an all-service economy would also be recession-free?" Why?

10. How do you account for the misconceptions concerning the service sector discussed on pp. 187 and 188?

Chapter 1

1. Based on your reading of the description of Carrefour on pp. 5 through 7, what business is the company in? How well does the company meet your definition of its service concept? What additional things might it consider to fulfill your definition even better?

2. Only recently have so-called warehouse food retailers in the U.S. built stores approaching the size of Carrefour. How do you explain this?

3. In the segmentation and targeting process for European airlines described on p. 9 of the text, are demographic or psychographic dimensions of the customer segment description more important? Why?

4. Describe a recent purchase of a service in which you experienced a high level of perceived risk. To what do you ascribe your feelings?

5. Why does auto repair generally rate so low on trustworthiness of the service?

6. Are there such things as commodity, nondifferentiable services? If so, what are some examples? How is your answer influenced by a reading of the examples on pp. 11 through 14?

7. Can you think of additional examples of ways in which service firms have sought successfully to serve the needs of two or more customer segments, as described on pp. 14 through 16?

8. How would you describe Wendy's International's service concept in terms of results produced for customers?

9. How do you explain the fact that several major airlines, in an effort to further focus their operating strategies, have adopted "hub-and-spoke" networks centered on smaller city hubs such as Charlotte, North Carolina and Salt Lake City, Utah?

10. Identify a business well-known in your community that you feel has focused its operating strategy well and indicate why you have selected it.

11. How does the Xerox Corporation's system for servicing and maintaining its equipment, described on pp. 20-22, support other elements of the firm's "service vision?" (In order to respond to this question, you will first have to make some assumptions about Xerox's target markets, its service concept, and some elements of its operating strategy.)

12. In what ways is the building in which you work designed to welcome, facilitate, intimidate, or discourage visitors? How important is this design to the success of the organization?

13. How does Shostack's "blueprinting" process for designing a service delivery system, illustrated in Figure 1-4, p. 24 of the book, relate

to questions raised in the diagram of the strategic service vision in Figure 1-1, p. 8?

Chapter 2

1. How would you describe the Shouldice Hospital's service concept, based on your reading of the example on pp. 27-29?

2. How is this service concept supported by other elements of the hospital's strategic service vision?

3. Using the brief description of the operating strategy for Mark Twain Bancshares presented on p. 19, what would you conclude about the effectiveness with which this bank has positioned itself against its competition?

4. Why is concept testing of the sort described on p. 32 so difficult? Why might it produce questionable results? Given your responses, why do service firms use concept testing in researching markets?

5. Think about the recent purchase of a service that you have made. To what extent did the so-called secondary factors discussed on p. 33 play a part in your purchase decision? Why?

6. How useful is the process leading to the mapping of competitors' positions illustrated in Figure 2-3 on p. 34? What other dimensions might have proven just as useful to Southwest Airlines in this example?

7. In what ways are customers' expectations about the quality of service they may receive in a particular service encounter influenced? Give some examples based on your personal experience.

8. How is value leveraged over cost at Shouldice Hospital? To what extent does it employ each of the devices described on pp. 37 through 42?

9. In what ways have you experienced efforts by service providers in recent months to manage your demands on them? Were they successful? Why?

10. To what extent has economic deregulation allowed airlines to manage demand and supply more effectively?

11. Why is quality control so difficult in a firm providing a so-called "high contact" service? How effective is direct supervision as opposed to other means of controlling quality likely to be in this kind of business?

12. What factors account for Rural/Metro Fire Department's ability to establish an advantage over its "competition," municipally managed fire protection, in the example described on pp. 42 and 43? To what

extent does this suggest possibilities for "privatizing" other
publicly managed services such as utilities, waste disposal services,
prisons, or police protection?

Chapter 3

1. Which of the basic or generic competitive strategies are Comp-U-Card,
   the Forum Corporation, and Burger King likely employing, based on the
   limited information provided on pp. 45 and 46 of the text?

2. What so-called "industry disadvantage" did each of these firms seek to
   overcome?

3. Describe a situation similar to examples presented in the book in
   which a company set itself apart competitively by converting a
   possible industry disadvantage to its own advantage.

4. In what ways does standardization of room design in its hotels help
   Holiday Inn lower its costs? Does this hinder or foster a competitive
   strategy that seeks to differentiate its service?

5. Based on the limited information given on pp. 48 and 49 about Hyatt
   Legal Services, how would you describe its service concept? Its
   service delivery system? What would you predict as characteristics of
   its operating strategy?

6. How would you reposition Mark Twain Bancshares and the three different
   types of outlets operated by Citibank on the customization-contact
   matrix shown in Figure 3-2 on p. 50?

7. What does Mastercard's retail credit card business have in common with
   firms described on pp. 51 through 53? Which of these firms would you
   expect to encounter a cost structure most similar to Mastercard? Why?

8. In Table 3-1, p. 52, contrast the profit models for Commonwealth
   Edison and Allied Van Lines. How did firms with such different profit
   models both manage to earn roughly comparable and reasonable returns
   on equity invested in 1984?

9. Obtain an annual report for a firm in the electric utility,
   transportation, or hospital services industries. Based on information
   in the annual report, calculate the firm's profit model for two or
   more years for which information is reported. How did the firm's
   profit model change from one year to the next? How did 1984
   performance compare with firms from its industry for which information
   is presented in Table 3-1, p. 52? How would you explain the
   differences between these firms' performances?

10. Would you expect more or less services to be delivered "off-line" in
    the future? Present some reasons, using examples to illustrate your
    argument.

11. Cite examples from your own experience of how intangible aspects of services have been made tangible. Was the effort to do so successful?

12. Which of the service-enhancing strategies discussed on pp. 54 through 59 generally takes the longest to implement? Which requires the most careful follow-up and continuing control? Why?

13. Cite an example in your experience in which a service strategy employing do-it-yourself customization was not successful. What reasons would you give for such results?

14. What are the risks associated with reducing individual judgment in the delivery process of a high-contact service? Draw upon your recent experience with a purchased service. How could the problem have been overcome in the example you cite?

15. Has the deregulation of many services led to more or less opportunity to manage supply and demand? Why? Illustrate your argument with specific industry examples.

16. How many "memberships," as described on pp. 63 and 64, do you "hold" in service delivery systems? Describe several of them. What benefits do you think these "memberships" offer to you? To the service firm you're patronizing?

17. Compare the asset- and people-intensity of Federal Express and Allied Van Lines, for which comparative data are presented in Table 3-1 on p. 52. Based on what you already know about these two firms, how do you explain the differences in their respective profit models?

18. How important are the potential problems of the "service triangle" for firms such as Hyatt Legal Services, described on pp. 48 and 49? How might they be overcome? What are some other services facing the same potential problems?

19. Which basic competitive strategies are employed in the Eastern Airlines' Shuttle and UPS' package delivery service, described on pp. 70 through 72? Which of the alternative strategic departures diagrammed in Figure 3-1 on p. 47 do each of these firms rely on heavily in the design and delivery of their respective services?

Chapter 4

1. Based on what you know about it, how would you define Tom Staton's business?

2. What additional service ventures would fit logically under the umbrella of your definition of Staton's business?

3. Why do well-managed firms such as the Marriott Corporation and Dun & Bradstreet go into businesses that are not central to their respective business definitions, as discussed on pp. 76 and 77?

4. How much overlap in customers targeted by leading financial service firms is suggested by the statistics presented in Figure 4-1 on p. 80?

5. What reasons would you advance to explain the overlap suggested in Figure 4-1?

6. Do you foresee any of the firms mentioned in Figure 4-1 becoming a "full-service" financial services provider to a significant portion of the customers for which data are presented in the figure? Why?

7. Based on what you know about it, how would you define American Airlines' business? Toward what market segment should a business defined this way be targeted?

8. What are the implications of the discussion of geographic focus on pp. 82 and 83 for a new fast-food restaurant operator hoping to develop a business to be competitive with McDonald's?

9. How should a company like the Ryder System organize the marketing of its services to: (1) customers renting or leasing trucks to move household goods from one point to another; (2) local firms in need of short-term local transport capacity; and (3) local firms desirous of leasing trucks for longer periods of time for long-haul transport use? What are the implications of each of these target markets for the company's truck service and maintenance operations?

10. Do you agree with the quote at the bottom of p. 84? Can you think of examples that either support or refute the notions it presents?

11. What role in the cast of characters described on p. 87 was John McCoy of Banc One (formerly City National Bank) playing in the vignette described on pp. 85 and 86?

12. Why might service firms place relatively heavier reliance on market testing of new ideas or "products" than manufacturers?

13. Why is "benchmark creep" or failure to follow up on the success or failure of new products so common in both service and manufacturing firms?

Chapter 5

1. Why doesn't the principle of focus, which might be used as a rationale for breaking jobs into their simplest components, lead to maximum productivity for many service jobs?

2. In what types of service situations are customers most comfortable with service employees who are performing recombined jobs involving two or more traditionally different types of roles, such as piloting a commercial airplane and handling passengers' baggage? In which are they least comfortable with the phenomenon? Why?

3. Cite the major differences in the task of controlling quality in a high-contact as opposed to a low-contact service. For which is direct supervision as a means of quality control likely to be most successful? Why?

4. Why does higher quality often cost less than lower quality in the delivery of a service?

5. What are the most important benefits of measuring both service levels and customer perceptions of quality, as does American Airlines in the example described on pp. 95 and 96?

6. For which service industries do John Dearden's caveats, presented on pp. 97 and 98, have the greatest relevance? For which do his warnings have the least relevance? Why?

7. Recently, hospitals have engaged in promotional efforts on or near Thanksgiving and Christmas holidays to encourage doctors and their patients to use otherwise empty beds by scheduling elective treatment at such times. How is this a form of cost control for such institutions?

8. For which firms (see Table 3-1 on p. 52) is asset control most important? Why? Speculate on how these firms have managed to reduce the asset intensity of their respective businesses.

9. In spite of the advice offered by Sasser on pp. 100 and 101, why do companies often establish the same labor control policies for all types of jobs? How could this pattern be broken where it might be desirable to do so?

10. Which of the service industries is likely to experience the greatest productivity gains from the introduction of new technologies that are already known to be in development? Which may experience the least? Why? (Having responded to this question, check your opinions against the data presented in Table C-1 on p. 192.)

Chapter 6

1. Which of the barriers to entry listed on p. 108 and discussed elsewhere in Chapter 6 are most important for firms in the life insurance industry? In the fast food chain restaurant industry? In real estate brokerage? Why?

2. What are the most important factors contributing to change in barriers to entry experienced by many service firms today?

3. How do concepts of "level" and "chase" strategies for managing capacity relate to those for controlling labor, discussed in Chapter 6?

4. Is a firm employing a "level" or "chase" demand strategy likely to achieve greater economies of scale by increasing its volume of business? Why?

5. Are there service industries other than passenger air transport where the "S-curve" described on pp. 110 and 111 is an important determinant of market share? Why have you selected each?

6. What is the most effective antidote to the type of competitive behavior that can arise among firms in industries in which the "S-curve" is important, raising levels of service or lowering prices? Why?

7. Cite examples of services you utilize in which your switching costs are high. In any of them, have attempts been made to increase your switching costs recently? Describe these efforts.

8. To what extent are network effects important today in the selection of a long-distance telephone service in the U.S.? In the selection of a real estate broker to handle the sale of your home? In the selection of a particular brand of traveller's checks? In the purchase of a hamburger? Why?

9. What implications do your responses to question 8 have for firms offering those services?

10. Given the value of the database at American Home Shield, described on p. 114, what new sources of revenue might this firm realize from the development of services utilizing this information?

11. Does the stock market tend to undervalue those service firms relying heavily on a valuable database for much of their competitive advantage? Why?

12. How is the balance of power in a supplier-customer relationship changed when a drug products distributor makes its inventory records directly accessible to a hospital's purchasing department by means of installing a computer terminal at the hospital? When a firm operating a fast-food chain estimates its demand several days in advance and communicates this information to one supplier from which it purchases all of its paper and meat products?

Chapter 7

1. A number of professional service firms, such as management consultancies, investment banking firms, and advertising agencies, have offered stock to the public recently. What are buyers of this stock acquiring? How would you contrast this with the purchase of stock in a mining or forest products company?

2. What are the major advantages of the "lean at the top" philosophy practiced by many successful service firms? What are some major disadvantages?

3. How do you reconcile a high degree of decentralization with the "tightly centralized system of policies, procedures, and controls" in the Marriott example presented on pp. 119 and 120?

4. Is coordination of operations and marketing more important in a computer-oriented consumer database service or a package pickup and delivery service? Why?

5. Why are field managers in multisite service firms so often found to be responsible for several functions, including operations and marketing? What does this suggest about the opportunity for general management (encompassing several functions) experience in such firms?

6. Why couldn't the Chase Manhattan Bank, N.A. have achieved the results described for its nonloan products just as easily by means other than creating product managers in the example presented on p. 122?

7. How is the nature of the employee selection process linked to a company's policies concerning term of employment, promotion from within, and personal development?

8. Why is a program for personal development so important at the Marriott Corporation? Could the same be said for a manufacturing company hiring skilled laborers for employment on its assembly lines? Why?

9. How are concepts of varied assignments in a professional service firm related to those of the "service triangle," described on pp. 68-70?

10. Why are employees of many of the firms mentioned in Chapter 7 not members of a national union? What role could a national union play in such firms?

11. How is a conservative approach to finance at Delta Airlines, mentioned on p. 130, related to other of the company's policies toward employees? How does this help explain the importance of conservation in the practice of many of the companies cited in Chapter 7?

12. Provide examples of legends commonly passed from one person to another in an organization of which you have been a member? What do these legends suggest about the culture of the organization?

13. How do you reconcile the findings of one research study of service worker alienation among Delta Airlines' flight attendants, mentioned on p. 134, with other of the company's personnel policies, including its careful selection of employees?

Chapter 8

1. What are possible reasons for the importance of foreign trade in services to the United States as opposed to other countries?

2. Were you surprised that in 1980 the United Kingdom, France, and Switzerland were ranked two, three, and four, respectively, in the amount of surplus derived from foreign trade in services, as shown in Table 8-1 on p. 140? What reasons could you advance for these results?

3. What relations, if any, do you see between data in Table 8-1, p. 140 and that in Table A-3, p. 184? Did this confirm your expectations? Why?

4. In a physical sense, how does foreign trade in services differ from that in goods?

5. The possible emergence of the "global product" with common design marketed everywhere in the world has been a topic of debate in recent years. Is this concept more feasible for services or goods? Why?

6. Why do all of the service industries with high proportions of non-U.S. revenues in their respective revenue bases, as discussed on p. 143, offer business as opposed to consumer services?

7. What relationships would you expect between trends in international travel, international trade in goods, and international trade in services? Why? Illustrate your arguments with examples.

8. For which nations is a GATT agreement guaranteeing certain freedoms in the foreign trade of services most important? Why?

9. An argument is presented in Appendix B, p. 185, that many service jobs are much more difficult to export than jobs in manufacturing. How do you reconcile this assertion with information concerning foreign trade in services presented in Chapter 8?

10. Are arguments for restricting trade in services reasonable? Are they understandable? Based on past experience with free trade agreements for goods, what steps will have to be taken if barriers to trade in services are to be lowered?

11. Discuss the relative difficulty of offering high- and low-customer contact services on a multinational basis.

12. Based on the experiences cited for McDonald's, Swissair, and Mister Minit, describe how you would design and deliver a multinational service of your choice.

Chapter 9

1. Has deregulation made it easier or more difficult for consumers to purchase services intelligently? Explain.

2. It seems clear that deregulation often facilitates both the creation of new services and companies and the demise of others. Is this as desirable in a consumer service such as air passenger transport as it is in a business-oriented service such as motor freight transport?

3. What effect has the deregulation of telephone service had on you personally? On balance, has this been favorable or not?

4. Why do labor unions continue to be a major voice arguing for regulation in the service industries?

5. If new technologies become more readily available to large and small competitors alike because of declining costs, on what basis will such firms compete, for example, in offering financial services such as banking?

6. How may new technologies influence managers of companies like Virginia Electric Power Company and American Airlines, cited on p. 159, in redefining these companies' service concepts?

7. In your own experience, in what ways have you observed information being substituted for assets in services you utilize regularly?

8. How do you account for the fact that the Scandinavian Airlines System, in the example on p. 162, began diverting some of its aircraft away from its Copenhagen hub at about the same time that many U.S. airlines began establishing hubs and operating most of their flights through them?

9. What benefits other than the avoidance of added investment might Consolidated Edison Company of New York have gained from its conservation (demarketing) campaign described in p. 163?

10. What are the implications of the tendency for service companies to diversify across industry boundaries, as shown in Figure 9-1, p. 165, for future levels of competition in these industries? For the quality of services offered to customers?

11. How do you relate concepts of customization of service, described on pp. 166 and 167, to those of economies of scale discussed earlier?

12. What types of regulations for the collection, transportation, and use of personal information do you feel should be enacted? Should affected service firms be given a voice in the shaping of these regulations? Affected consumers?

13. Does the first nation to deregulate a service industry such as telecommunications put itself in position of advantage or

disadvantage in relation to other nations? What are the implications of deregulation for the last nation to deregulate? Explain your responses to both questions.

14. How would you respond to the questions about the future posed on p. 172? Do you agree with the quote from Gartner and Riessman on the same page?

15. How is Daniel Bell's description of work in the service-oriented, postindustrial society as a "game between persons" as opposed to the industrial society's "game against fabricated nature" on p. 2 related to the comments of Gartner, Riessman, Cleveland, Nora, and Mine in Chapter 9?

Chapter 10

1. Does the growth of the service sector follow in time that of the goods-producing industries or vice-versa? Explain.

2. What are the implications of John Kendrick's prediction on p. 176? For example, relate this to the Marvin Harris quote on p. 2.

3. How do you explain differences between hypotheses about future job opportunities in services expressed by Marvin Harris on p. 2 and by the author on pp. 176 and 177?

4. In view of information presented in this book, how do you account for the quote attributed to the highly regarded, well-informed business leader, Lee Iacocca, on p. 187? What relevance does the discussion in Appendix C have to your explanation?

5. In what ways may a service economy help deliver the quality of life that Daniel Bell describes in the quote on p. 178?

COROLLARY MATERIALS

There is a growing body of materials on the subject of the management of service firms, particularly dealing with marketing and operations management. While much of it may have limited suitability for use in the classroom, this section sets forth listings of those readings, cases, and other resources that may be of greatest interest for instructional use.[1]

---

[1]All Harvard Business School cases, notes and Harvard Business Review reprints are available from the HBS Publishing Division. For your convenience an order form is included with this manual. Orders can also be placed by calling (617)495-6117 M-F, 9-5 EST.

Readings

Readings listed below are only the most applicable and the most readily available to the instructor. Many other possible readings for particular purposes can be found in the footnotes to the chapters of the book, including a number of interesting book-length efforts that purposely have not been listed again in this section.

General Articles

Levitt, Theodore, "Production-Line Approach to Service," Harvard Business Review, September/October 1972, HBR reprint no. 72505.

Levitt, Theodore, "The Industrialization of Service," Harvard Business Review, September/October 1976, HBR reprint no. 76506.

Maister, David H., "The Psychology of Waiting Lines," in The Service Encounter, John A. Czepiel, Michael R. Solomon, and Carol F. Surprerant, eds. (Lexington, Mass.: D.C. Heath, 1985).

Maister, David H., Note on the Management of Queues, HBS Case No. 9-680-053, 1979, 18 pp.

Thomas, Dan R.E., "Strategy is Different in Service Businesses," Harvard Business Review, July/August 1978, HBR reprint no. 78411.

Marketing Management

Berry, Leonard L., "Services Marketing is Different," Business, May-June, 1980.

Berry, Leonard L., "The Employee as Customer," Journal of Retail Banking, Vol. 3, No. 1, 1981.

George, William R. and Leonard L. Berry, "Guidelines for the Advertising of Services," Business Horizons, July/August 1981.

Lovelock, Christopher H., "Classifying Services to Gain Strategic Marketing Insights," Journal of Marketing, Summer 1983.

Lovelock, Christopher H. and Robert F. Young, "Look to Consumers to Increase Productivity," Harvard Business Review, May-June 1979, HBR reprint no. 79310.

Lovelock, Christopher H., "Why Marketing Management Needs to be Different for Services," in James H. Donnelly and William R. George, eds., Marketing of Services (Chicago: American Marketing Association, 1980).

Rice, James A., Richard S. Slack, and Pamela A. Garside, "Hospitals Can Learn Valuable Marketing Strategies from Hotels," Hospitals, November 16, 1981.

Sweet, Neesa, "The Fine Art of Franchising," Sky, February 1981, 11-16; 6 pp.

Operations Management

Chase, Richard B., "Where Does the Customer Fit in a Service Organization?", Harvard Business Review, November/December 1978, HBR reprint no. 78601.

Dearden, John, "Cost Accounting Comes to Service Industries," Harvard Business Review, September/October 1978, HBR reprint no. 78503.

Hostage, G. M., "Quality Control in a Service Business," Harvard Business Review, July/August 1975, HBR reprint no. 75405.

Maister, David H., "Balancing the Professional Service Firm," Sloan Management Review, Fall 1982.

Maister, David H. and Christopher H. Lovelock, "Managing Facilitator Services," Sloan Management Review, Summer 1982.

McFarlan, F. Warren, "Information Technology Changes the Way You Compete," Harvard Business Review, May/June 1984, HBR reprint no. 84308.

Mills, Peter K. and Dennis J. Moberg, "Perspectives on the Technology of Service Operations," Academy of Management Review, Vol. 7, No. 3, 1982.

Packer, Michael B., "Measuring the Intangible in Productivity," Technology Review, February-March 1983.

Sasser, W. Earl, Jr., "Match Supply and Demand in Service Industries," Harvard Business Review, November/December 1976, HBR reprint no. 76608.

Schneider, Benjamin, "The Service Organization: Climate is Crucial," Organizational Dynamics, Autumn 1980.

Schneider, Benjamin and David E. Bower, "New Services Design, Development and Implemenation and the Employee," in W. R. George and L. Marshall, eds., New Services (Chicago: American Marketing Association, 1985).

Skinner, Wickham, "The Focused Factory," Harvard Business Review, May/June 1974, HBR reprint no. 74308.

Cases

Cases are listed alphabetically by industry within the service sector. Each reference contains the case title, length, Harvard Business School case reference number, date of copyright, service industry categorization, primary business location, major topics covered in the case, HBS case teaching note reference number (if available), other supplementary

materials (such as videotapes), if available, and suggested questions for assignment in conjunction with the case.

While this is a relatively complete listing of available case materials on service firm management, it does not include cases of excessive age or those that, for other reasons, appear to be out of date. Several older cases highlighting classic, timeless issues are included.

Banking

Buffalo Savings Bank (A), 9-581-059 (1980)
Banking, U.S., service delivery system, (customer involvement), competitive positioning, technology, 22 pp.

Supplements: Teaching note, 5-585-065; videotape, 9-885-003

1. Identify all the alternative methods of delivery retail bank services to consumers.

2. What are the implications of each method for (a) customer satisfaction, and (b) operational efficiency?

3. What action should BSB take on Metroteller and Bank-and-Shop?

Buffalo Savings Bank (B), 9-581-060 (1981)
Banking, U.S., service delivery system (customer involvement), competitive positioning, technology, 3 pp.

Supplements: Teaching note, 5-585-065; videotape, 9-885-003

1. Assess the decisions concerning point-of-sale banking made by the management of the Buffalo Savings Bank.

2. What actions would you recommend to Warren Emblidge concerning Bank-and-Shop?

Chemical Bank (A), The Payments Automation Project, 9-485-178 (1985)
Banking, international, operating strategy (organization, entrepreneurship), marketing strategy, 18 pp.

Supplements: Videotape, 9-886-005

1.   What should Ms. Capsalis recommend at the meeting of the
     Operating Policy Committee?

2.   What data should she cite to support her recommendations?   Why?

Chemical Bank (B):   The Payments Automation Project, 9-485-029 (1984)
Banking, international, operating strategy (organization,
entrepreneurship, implementation), 14 pp.

Supplements: Videotape, 9-886-014

1.   What is your assessment of what Ms. Capsalis did?

2.   What should she do now?

First National City Bank Operating Group (A), 9-474-165 (1975)
Banking, international, operating strategy (organization, control,
staffing), service delivery system (technology), industrialization of
service, 11 pp.

Supplements: Teaching note, 5-483-053

1.   As Bob White, how enthusiastically would you welcome the
     opportunity to "take over Area I"?

2.   What would your program of action for Area I be?

First National City Bank Operating Group (B), 9-474-166 (1975)
Banking, international, operating strategy (implementation of new
technology), industrialization of service, 15 pp.

1.   Evaluate the process of "industrializing" the OPG at First
     National City Bank.

2.   What should John Reed's next actions be?

Manufacturers Hanover Corporation--Worldwide Network, 9-185-018 (1984)
Banking, international, 35 pp.

1.   What needs of an operation such as retail banking systems can
     GEONET meet?

2.   Outline an action plan for implementing the new network service.

Mark Twain Bancshares, Inc., 9-385-178 (1984)
Banking, U.S., multisite operating strategy (organization, control),
operating concept, market positioning, 25 pp.

Supplements: Videotape, 9-886-006

1.   Why has Mark Twain been successful?

2.   What forms have entrepreneurship and innovation taken at Mark Twain?

3.   What problems does the bank face in 1984?

4.   What recommendation would you make to Mr. Aronson for the St. Louis area banks? Should Mark Twain continue to expand, hold the number of banks constant, or consolidate? How should Mr. Aronson implement your recommendations?

Note on Payment Systems, 9-485-030 (1984)
Banking, U.S., 10 pp.

Communication, Information, and Media

AT&T Long Lines (A) Marketing Telemarketing, 9-580-145 (1980)
Communications, U.S., service concept, market positioning, marketing strategy, 30 pp.

Supplements: Teaching note, 5-581-157; videotape, 9-880-013

1.   What customer needs can Telemarketing meet? From the point of view of the customer, what is the Telemarketing "product"?

2.   How would you describe the decision-making unit and the decision-making process for Telemarketing?

3.   How can Mr. Wyman best relate to the National Account Teams in developing a complete marketing strategy?

4.   What specific recommendations would you make to Mr. Wyman? When should he start?

Business Research Corporation (A), 4-285-089 (1985)
Business information service, U.S., new venture start-up, finance, 30 pp. Special permission is required for use of this case.

1.   Which financing proposal should Bill Benjamin choose?

2.   Should Parker and his fellow investors put money into BRC?

Business Research Corporation (B), 4-285-090 (1985)
Business information service, U.S., new venture start-up, finance, 30 pp. Special permission is required for use of this case.

1. How <u>should</u> the capital structure be changed? How <u>will</u> the capital structure be changed?

2. Why does BRC need money? How much does it need? From whom should the money be raised? On what terms?

CompuServe (A) and **(A₁)**, 9-386-067 and 9-386-094 (1985)
Information services and communications, U.S., service concept, operating strategy (allocation of resources, executive compensation), 34 pp.

Supplements: Teaching note, 5-386-086

1. What actions would you advise Jeff Wilkins and Charlie McCall to take concerning the capital and expense budget requests for fiscal 1985? Why?

2. How, if at all, might Wilkins and McCall be influenced by the Executive Compensation Plan? Does this suggest any changes that should be made in the plan?

CompuServe (B), (C), (D), (E), 9-386-095, 9-386-096, 9-386-097, 9-386-098 (1985)
Information services and communications, U.S., operating strategy (management transition), 19, 3, 5, and 3 pp.

Supplements: Teaching note, 5-386-086

Assignment questions for the (B) case:

1. Should Charlie McCall take the job?

2. What are the potential problems facing him if he does accept the offered position?

3. What advice would you give McCall in dealing with these problems were he to accept the new position?

Independent Publishing Company, 9-377-062 (1976)
Newspaper publishing, U.S., operating strategy (cost control), service concept definition, service delivery system, 23 pp.

1. What problems does John Ginn face?

2. What should John Ginn do?

3. How should Bob Marbut evaluate John Ginn in this situation?

The Information Bank, 9-576-257 (1976)
Information services, U.S., service concept definition, market
positioning, marketing strategy (pricing), 26 pp.

1. As a member of the senior management of the New York Times
    Corporation, would you accept Mr. Keil's business objectives?
    Why?

2. Would you support continued investment in the Information Bank?
    For how long? How much would you be willing to invest in total?

KCTS-Channel 9, Seattle, 9-577-136 (1977)
Broadcast communications, U.S., competitive strategy, marketing
research, positioning, operating strategy, 25 pp.

Supplements: Teaching note, 5-578-063

1. Where should KCTS place its priorities in making programming
    selections for the current year? Why?

2. Evaluate the Viewers' Choice project as a vehicle for making
    these programming decisions.

Lotus Development Corporation, 4-285-094 (1985)
Microcomputer software, U.S., new venture start-up, finance, 32 pp.
Special permission is required for use of this case.

This case contains a description of a decision confronting Mitch
Kapor, founder of Lotus Development Corporation, in early 1982. He
must respond to an offer to provide financing by Sevin Rosen Partners,
a venture capital firm. Among the issues you might consider are the
following?

1. How should Kapor respond to L. J. Sevin?

2. Should Sevin Rosen invest in Lotus Development Corporation? If
    so, under what terms?

3. What should Kapor do?

Note on the Microcomputer Software Industry (January 1982), 9-285-095
(1985)
Microcomputer software industry, U.S., background information, 26 pp.

Note on the Newspaper Industry, 9-377-011 (1977)
Newspaper publishing, U.S., background material (service concept
design, competitive strategy), 30 pp.

1. What is a newspaper?

2. What are the most important trends in the newspaper industry?
    What are the implications of these trends?

3. If you were going to structure a company in the industry, how
    would you go about it?

The Saturday Evening Post, 9-373-009 (1972)
Publishing (magazine), U.S., market positioning, service concept,
operating strategy (organization, control), 19 pp.

1. Why was the Post successful?

2. Why did it die?

3. When did it begin to fail?

4. Could it have been saved? By whom and when?

STA Media, 4-285-147 (1985)
Film production, U.S., new venture start-up, finance, 14 pp. Special
permission is required for use of this case.

This case contains a description of a decison confronting Sam Tyler,
president of STA Media. Tyler has succeeded in gaining the rights to
produce a film based on In Search of Excellence, the bestselling book
by Tom Peters and Robert Waterman. Tyler needs to raise $250,000 to
finance the introduction of a series of products based on the film.
Among the issues you might consider are the following:

1. What is the nature of the opportunity confronting Sam Tyler, John
    Nathan, and STA Media?

2. How much money does STA need? From whom should the money be
    raised? On what terms?

3. What should Tyler do?

Technical Data Corporation, 4-283-072 (1983)
Data analysis services, U.S., new ventures start-up, finance, 29 pp.
Special permission is required for use of this case.

1. What is reasonable value for Technical Data Corporation?

2. What should Parker do?

Trade in Services and American Express, 9-383-114 (1983)
Information-based services, international, operating strategy
(external relations, stance on regulation), 21 pp.

1. How would you evaluate American Express' management's actions to date in opposing protectionism against trade in services?

2. What should the company's next step be?

Financial (Including Insurance)

David Marcus Backstage, 9-481-138 (1981)
Investment brokerage, U.S., operating strategy (personnel selection, job definition, productivity, quality control), 36 pp.

What can be learned from this story?

Hartford Steam Boiler Inspection and Insurance Company, 9-675-088 (1974)
Insurance, U.S., operating strategy (quality control, focused operating process), service delivery system design, 18 pp.

1. Why are policy lead times so long?

2. Assume the role of Donald Wilson, vice president for agency. What is your plan of action to correct the service-level problems facing HSB?

3. What are the major implementation problems facing Mr. Wilson? How should these problems be approached?

The Massachusetts Mutual Life Insurance Company, 9-182-276 (1982)
Insurance, U.S., service concept (product line planning), operating strategy (information systems), 35 pp.

1. Why does ISD play such an important role in the organization of this company?

2. What further action, if any, would you take to capitalize on information systems support at Massachusetts Mutual?

Mitchum, Jones & Templeton, 9-573-068 (1973)
Stock brokerage, U.S., positioning, service concept definition, operating strategy (broker hiring, training, compensation, and supervision), 8 pp.

Supplements: Videotape, 9-884-005

1. Where does the broker fit in a stockbrokerage organization from (a) an operations standpoint; (b) a marketing standpoint?

2. What broker hiring, training, compensation and supervision procedures do you recommend at MJT?

3. What action should MJT take concerning personal financial
    planning?

Progressive Corporation (A), 9-381-088 (1981)
Insurance underwriting (property-casualty), U.S., market positioning,
operating strategy (organization, control, leadership), 49 pp.

1. How would you describe Progressive's business strategy?

2. How does a company make money in this business?

3. What would you advise Peter Lewis to do?

Venture Capital Industry (1981), Note, 9-285-096 (1985)
Venture capital industry, U.S., background information, 38 pp.

Food and Lodging

Benihana of Tokyo, 9-673-057 (1972)
Restaurant, U.S., service concept definition, operating strategy,
service delivery system design, marketing, positioning, 16 pp.

Supplements: Teaching note, 5-677-037

1. How well thought out is the service delivery system (flows,
    inventories, etc.) of Benihana of Tokyo? (Assume the average
    time required to consume one drink is 20 minutes.)

2. To what extent have principles suggested by those advocating the
    "industrialization of services" been applied here?

3. What are the key ingredients in Benihana's business recipe?

4. Would you purchase a franchise from Benihana? In answering this
    question assume that you are a prospective franchisee examining
    the possibility of establishing a Benihana in Indianapolis,
    Indiana. It is estimated that you will have to invest about
    $300,000 in the building and its fixtures as well as pay the
    Benihana Corporation $20,000 for the training and transportation
    of personnel needed to maintain an adequate staff. The
    restaurant under consideration is similar in size and layout to
    the unit shown in Exhibit 2 of the case. The ongoing royalty
    under the agreement will be 8% of gross receipts. In return, the
    Benihana Corporation will retain responsibility for developing
    advertising campaigns for your local use, maintaining a supply of
    critical personnel (including chefs), and developing sources of
    distinctive supplies used in the operation.

Dobbs House (A), 9-673-058 (1972)
Restaurant chain, U.S., operating strategy, organization, business
turn-around, multisite management, 24 pp.

1. If Jerry McKenzie goes to Memphis, what should he do in the first
   month, six months, year? (Set priorities for management action.)

2. What do you believe will be McKenzie's greatest problem and what
   must he do to overcome it?

3. As Jerry McKenzie, would you take the job? Under what
   conditions?

Dobbs House (B), 9-673-059 (1972)
Restaurant chain, U.S., operating strategy, organization, business
turn-around, multisite management, 9 pp.

1. Evaluate Jerry McKenzie's performance in his first 20 months as
   general manager of Fast Foods.

Dunfey Hotels Corporation, 9-581-114 (1981)
Hotel company, U.S., operating strategy, organization, multisite
management, 18 pp.

Supplements: Teaching notes, 5-585-057, 5-585-122; videotape,
9-883-002

1. Has Dunfey achieved an appropriate division of responsibilities
   between corporate HQ and the individual units?

2. What do you see as the major advantages and disadvantages of the
   Dunfey planning process?

3. How transferable is the Dunfey planning process to (a) other
   lodging chains; (b) other multisite service operations?

The Lodging Industry, 9-680-116
Lodging, U.S., 54 pp.

Marriott's Rancho Las Palmas Resort, 9-581-084 (1981)
Hotel, U.S., market positioning, multisite operating strategy,
marketing, 28 pp.

Supplements: Teaching note, 5-585-058

1. Should Rancho Las Palmas (RLP) be seeking to position itself as a
   five-star resort?

2. Should Rancho Las Palmas be opened during the summer off-season?

3. What do you see as RLP's principal competitors?

4. What can the Marriott chain contribute to RLP and the hotel to the chain?

5. What action can RLP take to stimulate primary demand for the Coachella Valley as a destination resort?

6. What marketing strategy do you recommend to Mr. Small in 1980?

   (a) during the peak-season
   (b) during the shoulder season
   (c) during the summer

The Parker House (A), 9-580-151 (1980)
Hotel, U.S. segmentation, positioning, marketing, operating strategy, 22 pp.

Supplements: Teaching note, 5-585-073

1. Identify and evaluate the steps taken to date to reposition The Parker House.

2. How is The Parker House currently positioned against competing hotels? What are its strongest and weakest characteristics from the standpoint of the different market segments it seeks to serve?

3. What recommendations would you make to Dunfey management concerning:

   (a) the extent and scheduling of any future room renovations at The Parker House?
   (b) other product-related changes (if any)?
   (c) future pricing strategy?
   (d) future segmentation strategy?

The Parker House (B), 9-580-152 (1980)
Hotel, U.S., segmentation, positioning, marketing, operating strategy, 29 pp.

Supplements: Teaching note, 5-585-060

1. Evaluate the segmentation scheme employed by The Parker House.

2. What is the rationale for grouping The Parker House with the Berkshire Place and the Ambassador East (a) from a marketing perspective; (b) from an operations perspective?

3. What action should be taken on the Trans Am tour request for room bookings?

The Stanford Court (A), 9-680-009 (1979)
Lodging, U.S., multisite operating strategy, market positioning, service concept design. 24 pp.

Supplements: Teaching note, 5-681-093; videotape, 9-884-016

1. Identify the strategy of The Stanford Court. This analysis should consider the operating, financial, marketing, organizational, and other aspects.

2. What must The Stanford Court management do well to execute this strategy?

3. Analyze the Nassikas' management style. Compare it to the Wilkinson style.

4. What recommendations would you make to Nassikas about chain operations? What differences should be anticipated, and how should he manage them?

The Stanford Court (B), 9-680-010 (1979)
Lodging, U.S., operating strategy (control), 19 pp.

Supplements: Teaching note, 5-681-093

1. Evaluate the accounting and reporting system designed by Nothman. How could it be improved?

2. If you were in Nassikas' position, how would you manage Nothman? The controllership function?

The Stanford Court (C), 9-680-011 (1979)
Lodging, U.S., market positioning, marketing strategy, 29 pp.

Supplements: Teaching note, 5-681-093

1. Describe and appraise The Stanford Court's historical marketing strategy.

2. Is this strategy appropriate for the future of The Stanford Court in San Francisco? Is it adaptable for multisite operations? Is this dependent on the circumstances?

3. What alternative marketing plan(s) and budget(s) should be considered by The Stanford Court?

4. What marketing plan would you recommend? Why?

5. Based on the case, appraise Ron Krumpos' performance. Should he be made corporate marketing manager if The Stanford Court were to become a multisite operation?

The Stanford Court (D), 9-680-037 (1979)
Lodging, U.S., organization culture, multisite operating strategy,
14 pp.

Supplements: Teaching note, 5-681-093

1.   What is your analysis of the <u>implications</u> of the data on
     managerial styles, and personal and professional objectives for
     (1) the potential problems of the hotel as a single operation in
     the short and long run; and (2) the possible option of the hotel
     becoming a multisite operation?

Victoria Station Incorporated, 9-674-012 (1973)
Restaurant chain, U.S., operating strategy (control), market
positioning, 26 pp.

1.   What are the key elements of the Victoria Station operating
     concept?

2.   What are the critical elements of the company's cost structure?

3.   What is the capacity of a typical Victoria Station unit?
     Estimate break-even based on case data.

4.   What are the major problems facing Victoria Station in (1973?
     How should they be dealt with?

Victoria Station, (Stanford University) (1976)
Restaurant chain, U.S., competitive strategy, 39 pp.

1.   Outline a strategy to support management's goal to maintain
     Victoria Station's success in the face of more sophisticated
     competition.

Waffle House, Inc. (J), 9-672-101 (1972)
Restaurant chain, U.S., multisite operating strategy (organization,
control, management information system), service delivery system,
35 pp.

1.   Given the growth objectives of Waffle House, how would you answer
     the five questions posed by Joe Rogers, Jr., on page one of the
     case?

2.   Assume the role of a district manager. What are your major
     concerns? How would you spend a typical day?

3.   Assume the role of a unit manager. What are your major concerns?
     How would you spend a typical day?

4.   What is your advice to Joe Rogers, Sr.? Jr.?

Wendy's Old-Fashioned Hamburgers, 9-677-122 (1976)
Restaurant chain, U.S. market positioning, service concept, operating
strategy, service delivery system (franchising), 22 pp.

Supplements: Teaching note, 5-677-220

1.   From the standpoint of Mike Scharff, how would you appraise
     Wendy's program?

2.   As a member of Wendy's management, what recommendations would you
     make concerning the regional franchising strategy?

Industrial

Cunningham, Inc.:   Industrial Service Group, 9-581-022 (1981)
Industrial repair and maintenance, U.S., service concept definition,
sales, organization, 24 pp.

Supplements: Teaching note, 5-585-066

1.   How can ISG best compete profitably in the industrial repair and
     maintenance business?

2.   What specific tasks and responsibilities should be assigned to
     managers at each of the four levels of the ISG organization (head
     office, region, territory, service center)?

3.   What recommendations would you make to Mr. McDonald concerning
     the future structure of the ISG sales organization?

Harvey Plant, Ltd., 9-678-188 (1978)
Industrial rental service, United Kingdom, service concept definition,
operating strategy (organization, control), multisite management,
20 pp.

Supplements: Teaching note, 5-679-122

1.   What differences exist between the contract-hire and casual-hire
     businesses?

2.   What are the implications of this for how Lex should organize to
     market and run the operations of the Harvey division?

3.   If your answer to question 2 is different from Harvey's current
     organization, how would you begin to implement your suggested
     changes? What would you do first?

National Mine Service Company (A), 9-581-055 (1980)
Wholesaling, industrial maintenance and manufacturing, U.S., service
concept definition, operating strategy (organization), market
positioning, 21 pp.

Supplements: Teaching note, 5-583-131

1. What future strategy would you recommend for this company? Why?

2. Is the new organization appropriate to this strategy?

Triangle Maintenance Corp., 9-572-030 (1971)
Cleaning and security services, U.S., multisite operating strategy
(organization, control), market positioning, 21 pp.

1. Why has the company been unsuccessful in expanding its operations
    geographically?

2. What recommendations would you make to Mr. Fine concerning his
    brand management? (Among other things, prepare a job description
    for a branch manager, indicate the qualities you would look for
    in staffing such positions, and suggest a compensation level for
    the job.)

Medical

Beth Israel Hospital, Boston, 9-579-180 (1979)
Hospital, U.S., positioning, marketing, 22 pp.

Supplements: Teaching note, 5-581-008

1. Who makes decisions on choice of a hospital for obstetrical
    services? How might such decisions be influenced?

2. Evaluate the importance of obstetrics relative to other services
    in the Beth Israel product line.

3. What action should the BI take concerning its obstetrical
    services?

Health Systems, Inc., 9-580-115 (1980)
Professional services (medicine), U.S., multisite operating strategy
(control), 21 pp.

Supplements: Teaching note, 5-585-061

1. What are the requirements for success in implementing a
    branch-office strategy for a professional service firm?

2. What factors have made HSI successful?

3.   What recommendations would you make to Bob DeVore?

Loma Vista Hospital, (Stanford University) (1968)
Medical services, U.S., service concept, target market positioning,
operating concept (job definition, assignment), service delivery
system (layout), 32 pp.

1.   As Mike Haig, how will you handle the request for the additional
      nurse in the cardiac care unit?

2.   Outline a plan for Mr. Luthy to improve nurse staffing procedures
      for the longer term. Keep in mind the rapidly increasing
      operating losses.

Max Able Medical Clinic (AR), 9-676-179 (1976)
Medical services, U.S., technology, automation, service delivery
system design, 23 pp.

Supplements: Teaching notes, 5-677-100, 5-678-071

1.   What is your analysis of the options facing Dr. Eugene?

2.   What recommendation would you make? Why?

Shouldice Hospital Limited, 9-683-068 (1983)
Hospital, Canada, positioning, service concept definition, operating
strategy, service delivery system design, capacity planning,
demand-supply management, 22 pp.

1.   Evaluate the target market, service concept, operating strategy,
      and service delivery system of Shouldice Hosptial. How well are
      they coordinated?

2.   What actions, if any, would you recommend that Dr. Shouldice take
      to increase the hospital's capacity?

3.   How would you implement the changes that you propose?

University Health Service: Walk-In Clinic, 9-681-061 (1981)
Medical services, U.S., service delivery system design, capacity
planning, queue management, 17 pp.

Supplements: Teaching note, 5-681-079

1.   Evaluate the performance of the Walk-In Clinic. Are waiting
      times now acceptable?

2.   Why are "walk-in appointments" a problem? What should Kathryn
      Angell do about them, if anything?

3.   What other actions, if any, would you recommend to Angell?

Professional

Comprehensive Accounting Corporation (1982), 9-585-123 (1984)
Accounting, U.S., multisite operating strategy (control), franchising,
marketing strategy, 24 pp.

1.   What are the requirements for success in a franchise service
     business?

2.   What factors have made Comprehensive Accounting successful?   Is
     it realistic to expect this success to continue?

3.   What recommendations would you make to the Lauzens?

Engineering Employment Exchange, Inc., 9-685-382 (1985)
Professional services (placement), U.S., positioning, service concept
definition, operating strategy (staffing, compensation, organization
structure), productivity, 23 pp.

1.   What is the firm's service concept?   How does it differ from
     other (traditional) employment agencies?

2.   What are the possible causes of the productivity problem at the
     firm?

3.   What recommendations for change, if any, would you make?   For the
     short term (up to one year)?   For the medium to long term?

Francis, Berther and Allfreed, 9-681-060 (1980)
Professional services (advertising agency) U.S., account management
and project team management,   20 pp.

Supplements: Teaching notes, 5-682-013, 5-682-009

1.   Why did the PERQUE campaign run into trouble?   Who was to blame?

2.   Evalaute FBA's systems and procedures.   Could improvements in
     these areas have prevented this problem?

3.   What options are now open to Max Lewis?   What would you do in his
     position?

Harris-Johnson Associates, 9-580-158,
Professional services (architect), U.S., positioning, service concept
definition, marketing, 17 pp.

Supplements: Teaching note, 5-585-059

1.   What is the architect's product?

2.   What are the principal market segments? In each instance, what
     is good service?

3.   As Beth Brigham, what do you recommend and how would you present
     your analysis and recommendations to Messrs. Harris and Johnson?

Hewitt Associates, 9-681-063 (1981)
Professional services (human resource management), U.S., operating
strategy (organization, control, personnel selection, human resource
development, job definition), 22 pp.

Supplements: Teaching notes, 5-682-015, 5-682-009

1.   Can Hewitt Associates continue to balance its three goals as it
     grows?

2.   What are the causes of the problems between professional groups
     and account managers?

3.   What changes, if any, in Hewitt's management systems would you
     recommend to Mr. Friedes?

The Law Offices of Lewin & Associates, 9-583-122 (1983)
Professional services (legal), U.S., operating strategy
(compensation), service concept, service delivery system, 18 pp.

1.   Do you agree with the statement (p. 2) that L&A is "in law what
     family practitioners are in medicine"? Why? Why not? (Consider
     the operations concept, service delivery system, service
     concept.)

2.   Evaluate the proposed new compensation scheme at L&A. Can
     anything useful be learned at L&A from the McDonald's experience?

3.   What recommendations would you make to Elizabeth Lewin? (Be
     prepared to open with these.)

Managing the Professional Service Firm: Module Teaching note,
5-682-009 (1981)
This note contains a module overview as well as teaching notes for the
cases: Scientific Placement, Inc.; Francis, Berther & Allfreed;
Spanglett Associates; Smith Jones; and Hewitt Associates, 27 pp.

Smith Jones, 9-681-072 (1981)
Professional services (accounting), U.S., operating strategy (employee assignment, selection, development, compensation, organization, control), 24 pp.

Supplements: Teaching notes, 5-682-009, 5-682-016

1.   Evaluate Smith Jones's process for assigning individuals to audit engagements.

2.   What changes would you suggest in the process? Why?

Spanglett Associates, 9-681-080 (1981)
Professional services (management consulting), U.S., operating strategy (employee assignment, development), service delivery system design (capacity planning), client relations, 16 pp.

Supplements: Teaching note, 9-682-009

1.   What are the major components of Spanglett's assignment system? What are they designed to accomplish?

2.   How does the assignment system relate to other management systems in the firm?

3.   What should Mr. Temple do about Mr. Stone?

The Architects Collaborative, Inc., 9-575-016 (1975)
Professional services (architectural), U.S., marketing, competitive positioning, service concept, operating strategy (organization, control), 28 pp.

Supplements: Teaching note, 5-581-070

1.   Why did TAC lose the Salisbury bid?

2.   What are TAC's strengths and weaknesses in comparison with CRS?

3.   Would you attempt to alter TAC's comparative strengths in fashioning a future strategy for the company? Why?

Public

Massachusetts State Lottery (A), (Northeastern University) (1972)
Public service, U.S., market positioning, product development, marketing research, service concept definition, 22 pp.

1.   What are some of the major determinants of the demand for lottery tickets?

2. What is the nature of the "product" being sold by the state?

3. What information is needed to support marketing decisions that must be made by the state?

4. How much of this information is available from the other three neighboring states already offering a lottery?

5. What plan of action would you recommend to the Lottery's director?

Rural Metro Fire Department, 9-681-082 (1981)
Fire protection service, U.S., positioning, service concept definition, multisite, operating strategy, service delivery system design, 27 pp.

1. Why has Rural Metro been successful in Scottsdale?

2. Can this company successfully expand on a multisite basis?

3. What key management tasks would be involved in developing and operating branches, and what skills would be required?

4. What short-term actions would you recommend to the new management team?

The 911 Emergency Number in New York, 9-575-099 (1975)
Public service, U.S., marketing strategy, service concept definition, 8 pp.

1. What elements would you suggest for a program to discourage unnecessary use of the 911 number? Why? (Make sure your response addresses the questions on the last page of the cases.)

U.S. Postal Service: Postal Money Orders, 9-575-088 (1975)
Public Service, marketing strategy, pricing strategy, 17 pp.

Supplements: Teaching note, 5-577-175

Recreation and Arts

American Repertory Theatre, 9-580-133 (1981)
Theatre, U.S., positioning, marketing, marketing research, pricing, advertising and selling, 28 pp.

Supplements: Teaching note, 5-585-062

1. What do you consider to be the key insights gained from ART's marketing research efforts?

2. Describe the specific elements of a subscription campaign including pricing and communications strategy, for ART's first season.

Bridger Bowl, Inc. (A), (Montana State University) (1975)
Ski resort, U.S., competitive positioning, marketing, operating strategy, 16 pp.

1. What should Bob Macdonald suggest to the directors concerning Bridger Bowl's expansion?

2. What other recommendations should he make for the upcoming season?

Lyric Dinner Theater (A), 9-386-056 (1985)
Entertainment, U.S., target market, service concept definition, operating strategy (organization, control), turn-around management, 21 pp.

Supplements: Videotape, 9-886-023

1. What is your assessment of Deborah Denenberg's performance to date?

2. What are the problems facing her? What priority would you assign to each?

3. What actions should Ms. Denenberg take? In what order?

Lyric Dinner Theater (B), 9-386-057 (1985)
Entertainment, U.S., operating strategy (organization, personnel selection and development, cost control, quality control), turn-around management, 7 pp.

1. Appraise Deborah Denenberg's performance in her first full year as general manager.

2. Should she begin looking for another position? Why?

The Sea Pines Racquet Club, 9-674-011 (1973)
Recreational services, U.S., service concept definition, service delivery system design (capacity planning), 14 pp.

Supplements: Teaching note, 5-677-038

1. What is the dilemma facing John Baker? What are his options?

2. How many tennis courts will be needed in July 1974? How does that requirement compare to present capacity?

3. What should he do for the upcoming season? For the next year?

4. What are the implications for John Baker regarding the future of tennis at Sea Pines?

Six Flags, Incorporated, 9-173-141 (1973)
Recreation (theme park), U.S., multisite operating strategy (control, organization), 21 pp.

1. As a consultant to John Berthold, outline changes you would suggest in the Six Flags management control system to enable the company to manage other amusement parks.

Vail Associates, Inc., 9-374-031 (1973)
Recreation (ski resort), U.S., service concept design, operating strategy (lease vs. sale of assets, quality control), 34 pp.

1. Should the management of Vail Associates exercise its option on the Beaver Creek property? Why?

2. What plan would you propose for implementing the strategy implied by your response to the first question?

Trade (Including Retailing and Wholesaling)

Benetton (A), 9-685-014 (1984)
Retailing, Europe, marketing strategy (new market development, pricing, product policy), franchising, operating strategy (personnel selection), service delivery system design (location, channels of distribution), 28 pp.

Supplements: Teaching note, 5-686-019; videotape, 9-886-010, "Benetton Plant Tour"

1. What are the most important elements of Benetton's marketing, logistics, manufacturing, and financial strategies?

2. How does it gain advantage over its competition in Europe?

3. Which of these important elements of strategy and sources of competitive advantage can it maintain in the U.S. market?

4. Would you introduce Benetton to the U.S. at this time (1982)? Why?

5. If so, how would you resolve questions posed in the case? What other questions might you address?

Benetton (B), 9-685-020 (1985)
Retailing, Europe and the U.S., marketing strategy (new market
development), franchising, operating strategy (organization, control),
26 pp.

1. What should Aldo Palmeri's agenda be? In what order should he
   address these items? In what manner?

2. Should Benetton establish a separate U.S. subsidiary? Why?

Carrefour S.A., 9-273-099 (1973)
Retailing, France, operating strategy (new market development),
service concept, market positioning, finance, 12 pp.

1. How do needs of customers and suppliers as well as the
   competitive environments of France and the United States compare?

2. What implications does this have for a possible expansion by
   Carrefour to North America? Would you recommend the expansion?

Hills Department Stores, 9-577-024 (1976)
Retailing, U.S., operating strategy (product-line planning), 34 pp.

1. What is Hills doing right?

2. How does it compare with other DDSs?

3. Are all elements of Hills' operating strategy consistent?

4. Should Hills experiment with a smaller unit format?

L.L. Bean, Inc.: Corporate Strategy, 9-581-159 (1981)
Retailing, U.S., market definition, service concept, operating
strategy (organization, rate of growth), 35 pp.

1. Appraise L.L. Bean in terms of basic and integrative elements of
   the strategic service vision?

2. How would you advise Mr. Gorman on the issues stated at the end
   of the case?

Marks and Spencer, Ltd. (A), 9-375-358 (1975)
retailing, United Kingdom, service concept, competitive positioning,
operating strategy, 33 pp.

1. How successful is Marks and Spencer?

2. How do you account for this result?

3.   What problems does the company face in the future?

4.   How would you propose they be resolved?

Paper Distributors, Inc. (A) and **(B)**, 9-576-022 and 9-576-023 (1975)
Wholesaling, U.S., marketing strategy, sales management, operating
strategy (personnel selection, development, control), 8 and 14 pp.

1.   Evaluate Frank Hatch. What are his strengths and weaknesses?
      Motivations?

2.   How would you help him improve his performance?

3.   How do PDI's sales force management policies help or hinder Frank
      Hatch's improvement?

Mitsubishi Corporation (A), 9-482-050 (1981)
Wholesaling and manufacturing (trading company), Japan, operating
strategy, competitive positioning, finance, 35 pp.

Supplements: Videotape, 9-884-015

1.   What do you see in this case that surprises you?

2.   What are the competitive threats and strategic issues for the
      Mitsubishi Corporation in 1981? How should the corporation's
      management begin to address the issues?

Mitsubishi Corporation (B), 9-482-051 (1981)
Wholesaling and manufacturing (trading company), Japan, multinational,
operating strategy (organization, control), 30 pp.

Supplements: Background reading: "Mitsubishi, A Japanese Grant:
                Plans for Growth in the U.S.," Business Week, 20 July
                1981, pp. 128-132

1.   How does the "Americanization" of MIC relate to the strategic
      issues faced by the parent that were discussed in the (A) case?

2.   What are the costs and benefits of "Americanization" from the
      point of view of the MIC's general managers? From the point of
      view of Mitsubishi's corporate management in Japan?

3.   What should corporate management do?

Sears, Roebuck & Co. in the '80s (A), 9-386-029 (1985)
Retailing and financial services, U.S., service concept, competitive
strategy, operating strategy (integrating an acquisition), 25 pp.

1. Based on your knowledge of Sears and Dean Witter, how, if at all, can the latter be integrated into Sears' financial services strategy?

2. Create an action plan for implementing the new strategy. How, it at all, can the expected synergies be created? How much and in what areas should Sears' management intervene? Is it important to create a single "Sears way"?

Supermarket Services, Inc. (SMS), 9-577-091 (1977)
Wholesaling (rack jobbing), U.S., marketing strategy, product development, service concept, operating strtegy, 30 pp.

1. What does SMS' "cost plus" program do for a retailer?

2. Should SMS continue its "cost plus" program? Why?

3. Assuming the program is to be continued, what modifications, if any, would you recommend in it?

Transportation

British Airways, 9-585-014 (1984)
Passenger transportation (airline), international, marketing strategy (global advertising), operating concept, market positioning, 28 pp.

1. How is the market for air travel segmented? How do consumers choose which airline to use?

2. Why has BA decided to invest in a corporate image campaign worldwide?

3. Does a global marketing campaign make sense for BA? For which types of services is global marketing relevant?

4. What implementation problems face BA in trying to execute a global advertising campaign? How can these be overcome?

Burnham Van Service, Inc., 9-581-065 (1980)
Freight transportation (household goods), U.S., positioning, marketing strategy, service concept definition, 25 pp.

Supplements: Teaching note, 5-585-063

1. What recommendation would you make to Mr. Crowley concerning the issue of specialization?

2. What effect does the deregulated environment for the trucking

industry have on your recommendation?

Continental Airlines (A), 9-385-006 (1984)
Passenger transportation (airline), U.S., turn-around management,
operating strategy (cost control, labor relations), 32 pp.

Supplements: Videotape, 9-885-012

1.   What should Frank Lorenzo do concerning new business
     opportunities in the South Pacific? Why?

2.   What constituencies will have to be managed to get the new
     routes? How should this be done?

Continental Airlines (B), 9-385-007 (1984)
Passenger transportation (airline), U.S., turn-around management,
operating strategy (external relations, labor relations), 37 pp.

1.   Is Frank Lorenzo managing this turn-around so that his company is
     coming out of it in the desired way? Be specific in your
     response.

FBO, Inc., 9-678-117 (1978)
Aircraft ground services company, U.S., service delivery system,
operations planning, control, equipment and personnel scheduling,
capacity planning, 17 pp.

1.   How well is FBO's existing scheduling system for refueling
     operations working at Metro Airport?

2.   What are ways to improve the existing pooling concept?

3.   Evaluate the alternatives being considered by Mr. Reiling.

4.   Develop a plan of action for Mr. Reiling, including an
     implementation scheme.

     (The case involves quite a high degree of numerical analysis. In
     order to limit preparation time, it may be advisable to add the
     following questions as guidance.)

5.   Construct an income statement for FBO.

6.   Develop a schedule for the time period 6:30 a.m.-12 noon. How
     many vehicles are needed?

7.   Estimate the utilization of available manpower and of available

equipment. What conclusions do you draw from this analysis?

8. List and consider the "rules of thumb" that FBO appears to use in the management of its operations. Do you agree with them? Can you develop any others that would better assist operations planning and control?

Federal Express (A), 9-577-042 (1976)
Freight transportation, U.S., marketing strategy (advertising, selling), operating strategy, service delivery system, 26 pp.

Supplements: Teaching note, 5-577-189

1. How much would you spend on a promotional program for Courier Pak?

2. How would you spend the budget you purpose? Be specific.

3. What implications does your promotional program have for Federal Express' operating strategy?

Federal Express Customer Service Department (A), 9-581-017 (1980)
Freight transportation, U.S., multisite operating strategy, service delivery system design,   20 pp.

Supplements: Teaching note, 5-585-064; videotape, 9-883-001

1. Prepare a diagram identifying all the different ways in which customers interact with Federal Express.

2. Evaluate the company's decision to set up a separate Customer Service Department. How should this department relate to (a) sales; and (b) operations?

Federal Express Customer Service Department (B), 9-581-102 (1981)
Freight transportation, U.S., delivery system design, marketing, operating strategy, 11 pp.

Supplements: Teaching note, 5-585-064

1. How should Heinz Adam respond to the concerns expressed by operations and sales personnel in relation to COSMOS?

Illinois Central Gulf Railroad, 9-583-083 (1982)
Freight transportation, U.S., marketing strategy (promotional effort, telemarketing), 33 pp.

1. Does Harry Bruce's proposal represent the right way to compete in the railroad business?

2. Should Bruce's proposal be adopted on a national basis, tested regionally, or dropped?

3. How would you manage the human relations problems resulting from implementing your decision on question 2 above?

Medibus, Inc., 9-675-177 (1975)
Transportation (medical patients), U.S., operating strategy, service delivery system design, marketing, positioning, service concept definition, 26 pp.

1. Assuming an average speed of 30 m.p.h., examine the operational economics of Medibus.

2. How well is Medibus' operation designed to meet the needs of its market?

3. What changes, if any, do you recommend for the short-term future?

North American Van Lines, 9-675-149 (1975)
Household goods transport, U.S., operating strategy (capacity planning, subcontracting services), service delivery system, 16 pp.

Supplements: Teaching note, 5-677-114

1. What are the key factors NAVL (as the central organization) must concentrate on for success?

2. What is a reasonable assessment of stockout costs if NAVL is unable to accommodate a committed pick-up? Is 92 percent stockout coverage justified?

3. Analyze the traffic lanes between Regions 1 and 10 and Regions 1 and 4. How many trailers should be assigned during the main season? Assume fully loaded or fully empty trailers are operated. The average trailer contains three shipments.

4. Assuming that owner-operators speak to each other, what is a practical operating plan?

5. What do you recommend Walt Moore do?

People Express, 9-483-103 (1983)
Passenger transportation (airline), U.S., operating strategy

(organization, employee selection and development, control), 22 pp.

Supplements: Teaching note, 5-486-004; Videotapes, 9-885-015, 9-885-016

1. What are the most important elements of People Express' operating strategy?

2. How transferable is this operating strategy to other service firms?

3. How important is it for the future?

Ryder System, Inc. (B), 9-573-043 (1973)
Vehicle rental and leasing, U.S., product portfolio, operating strategy (organization, control), marketing, 18 pp.

1. How is the market for Ryder's service segmented?

2. How should Ryder organize to implement its marketing and associated operating strategies most effectively?

Scandinavian Airlines System, (Prof. Dean Berry, London Business School) (1983)
Passenger transport (airline), international, competitive positioning, service concept definition, operating strategy, 43 pp.

1. What was the situation facing Carlzon and what priorities would you place on the problems he faced?

2. What did Carlzon do that was most important? Why?

3. Were his actions taken in the proper sequence?

Singapore Airlines (A), 9-682-064 (1982)
Passenger transportation (airline), international, service concept design, operating strategy (employee selection, training), 7 pp.

1. How do you account for Singapore Airlines' "paltry" performance?

2. Is it what you would expect, based on Mr. Pillay's operating philosophy?

Singapore Airlines (B), 9-682-065 (1982)
Passenger transportation (airline), international, market positioning, marketing (advertising), service concept design, operating strategy (employee, selection, training, control), 24 pp.

1. How would you describe Singapore Airlines' service concept and operating strategy?

2. What is the "Singapore Girls" program? Should it be dropped?

Southwest Airlines (A), 9-575-060 (1975)
Passenger transportation (airline), U.S., market position, service concept definition, marketing strategy (pricing, product, advertising), service delivery system, 33 pp.

Supplements: Teaching note, 5-575-134; videotape, 9-883-010

1. What were the major problems facing Southwest Airlines in early 1971?

2. How had they changed by February 1, 1973?

3. What response, if any, should Southwest make to Braniff's "half-price sale"? Why?

Miscellaneous

Access, (LBS-M89, London Business School) (1985)
Advertising and value exchange (credit card), 35 pp.

1. What strategy should Sean MacShane's account team propose for the Access account?

2. How does this proposed strategy reflect the nature of the Access service concept and operating strategy?

American Home Shield Corporation, 9-673-110 (1973)
Home maintenance service, U.S., service concept definition, operating strategy, delivery system design, 22 pp.

1. What are the major market segments for AHS? How does each behave? How effective is the AHS delivery system for serving each segment?

2. What are the major factors affecting AHS's gross margins?

3. What questions would you raise as a member of the board of directors of this company at its March 20, 1973 meeting?

Bradford Schools, 9-681-049 (1980)
Commercial educational institution, U.S., service concept definition, marketing, operating strategy, service delivery system design, multisite management, quality control, operating control, 23 pp.

Supplements: Teaching note, 5-681-075

1.   What is a good secretary?

2.   What is good service in secretarial training?

3.   How can Bradford measure, monitor, communicate, and raise its
     service level?

Clark University (A), (Harvard University Institute for Educational
Management) (1973)
Educational institution, U.S., marketing strategy, service concept,
operating strategy (curriculum), 23 pp.

1.   What is the target market for Clark University?

2.   How, if at all, should Clark's offering be changed to meet the
     needs of its target market? Do the proposals for academic reform
     meet your proposals?

3.   What implications do the proposed academic reforms have for
     Clark's operating strategy?

Clark University (B), (Harvard University Institute for Educational
Management) (1974)
Educational institution, U.S., operating strategy, 2 pp.

1.   As an adviser to the new president of Clark, what program of
     action would you propose for implementing the academic reforms?

Consolidated Edison (A) and (B), 9-380-076 (1979)
Utility, U.S., operating strategy (finance, investment, constituent
relations), marketing strategy (demarketing), 22 pp.

1.   What are the most important problems facing Mr. Luce? What are
     the sources of these problems?

2.   What should Mr. Luce do in dealing with these problems? Should
     the quarterly dividend be omitted?

Consolidated Edison (C), 9-375-131 (1974)
Utility, U.S., operating strategy (constituent relations, finance,
investment), 3 pp.

1.   Do you support the shareholders' calls for Mr. Luce's
     resignation? Why?

Flair, Inc., 9-676-094 (1975)
Hairdressing, U.S., new venture start-up, industrializing a service,
service concept, staffing, operating strategy, incentives, service
delivery system, "service triangle", 18 pp.

1. Evaluate the Flair concept and business plan.

2. Carefully analyze the projected earnings of a company-owned salon
    in Exhibit 2 of the case. Do you agree with the projections?

3. Where can you apply production line techniques in the hair
    styling business? Where can't you?

4. What recommendations would you make to Matt Laidlaw and George
    Brimwell?

Garber Travel Services, Inc., 9-677-210 (1977)
Travel service, U.S., positioning, service concept definition,
operating strategy (selection, organization), service delivery system
design (location), 24 pp.

Supplements: Teaching note, 5-681-097

1. Which of the two candidates, if either, should Joan Gordon hire
    to manage the Cambridge office? Why?

2. To what extent does Gordon's choice depend on the positioning and
    operating strategy for the office? Explain.

3. What other recommendations would you make to Gordon concerning
    the organization and control of the Cambridge office?

Levinson Realty, Inc., 9-680-093 (1979)
Real estate brokerage, U.S., positioning, service concept, multisite
operating strategy (branch functions, control, organization), 22 pp.

1. What should Mike Rowebottom do? In the short term? In the long
    term?

2. What does it mean for a real estate firm to be "upmarket" and
    "seller-oriented"? How does this affect how Levinson should be
    organized?

Lex Service Group (A), 9-382-067 (1972)
Auto repair, United Kingdom, service concept definition, service
quality control, performance measurement, 17 pp.

1. What steps does a customer go through in getting a car serviced?

2. Evaluate Lex's attempts to define what is meant by good service.

3.   According to the survey in Exhibit 4, is service better at
     Cheltenham or Kidderminster?

Lex Service Group (B), 9-382-068 (1972)
Auto repair, United Kingdom, service concept implementation,
performance measurement, 10 pp.

1.   How should Lex resolve the trade-off between increased customer
     service and increased operating cost? How can this trade-off be
     managed?

2.   What are the characteristics needed by Lex for an effective
     branch manager?

Man of the House, Inc., 9-575-137 (1975)
Maintenance (home) service, U.S., market positioning, service concept
definition, product line development, marketing strategy, multisite
operating strategy, 32 pp.

1.   Recommend a marketing program to Mr. Weinstein.

2.   What suggestions would you make for the development of the
     company's branches?

Safecard Services, Inc., 9-673-096 (1973)
Credit card holder service, U.S., service concept definition,
marketing, operations planning, 30 pp.

1.   What is the Safecard service concept?

2.   What recommendations do you have for the Halmos brothers?

Turner Construction Company, 9-585-031 (1985)
Construction, U.S., marketing strategy, operating strategy
(organization, control, capacity planning), 21 pp.

1.   What is it like to be a general manager at Turner Construction
     Company?

2.   Is this a major or minor problem?

3.   What should Mr. Kupfer do? Why?

VISA International: The Management of Change, 9-482-022 (1981)
Value exchange (credit card) service, international, operating
strategy (organization, control, leadership), 43 pp.

1. Has Dee Hock and the management correctly defined VISA's service concept?

2. What should his agenda be for future changes in response to VISA's changing competitive environment?

Your School: _____ (final assignment for a formal academic course)

1. Describe your school in terms of its:

    1.1 Target market
    1.2 Service concept
    1.3 Operating strategy
    1.4 Service delivery system

2. Evaluate your school on each of the dimensions in question 1.

3. Based on your study of this course, what recommendations would you make to the administration of your school to increase the effectiveness of the institution?

SAMPLE COURSE OUTLINES

This section contains a number of course outlines, selected from materials referenced above and based on experience with the design of courses for both academic institutions and executive programs. Outlines for academic courses of one semester (45 classes) or one quarter (30 classes) in length are presented first. These include courses in management of services, services marketing, and management of service operations.

Executive program outlines are organized in terms of their constituency, with cross-industry courses listed first, followed by outlines for short, institutionally focused courses.

Each outline comprises listings of assignments by class number. The lists are intended to provide basic material for the preparation of course syllabi. References to the "text" chapters are those contained in Managing in the Service Economy. Questions for possible assignment in connection with both the text chapters and cases are presented above.

For your convenience all Harvard Business School cases and Harvard Business Review reprints listed under the sample course outlines in this handbook can be ordered using one number. See the enclosed order form. Teaching notes and videotapes must be ordered separately.

Management of Services: Semester Course, 9-200-100 or Quarter Course, 9-200-101

This set of assignments assumes a semester-length course of 45 sessions. Those specific items marked with an asterisk may be eliminated to create a quarter-length course of 30 classes. The assignments purposely have been designed to be ample. Those desiring to reduce the length of each assignment might eliminate certain of the assigned readings outside the text.

Introduction: The Strategic Service Vision

1. Lecture/Discussion
    Reading: Text, Introduction, Chapter 1 and Appendices A and B

2. Case: Benihana of Tokyo*, 9-673-057
          (TN: 5-677-037)

3. Case: Shouldice Hospital Limited, 9-683-068
    Reading: Text, Chapter 2

Defining the Service Concept

4. Cases: Lex Service Group (A) and (B), 9-382-067 and 9-382-068

5. Case: L. L. Bean, Inc.: Corporate Strategy,* 9-581-159

6. Case: AT&T Long Lines (A) Marketing Telemarketing*, 9-580-145
          (Video: 9-880-013; TN: 5-581-157)

7. Lecture/Discussion
    Reading: Lovelock, "Classifying Services to Gain Strategic
              Insight"

8. Case: Garber Travel Services, Inc., 9-677-210
          (TN: 5-681-097)

Positioning the Service Business

9. Lecture/Discussion
    Reading, Text, Chapter 3

10. Case: Southwest Airlines (A), 9-575-060
           (Video: 9-883-010; TN: 5-575-134)

11. Case: The Parker House (A), 9-580-151
           (TN: 5-585-060)

12. Case: The Architects Collaborative, Inc.*, 9-575-016
           (TN: 5-581-070)
     Reading: Lovelock, "Why Marketing Management Needs to be
               Different for Services"

Developing the Operating Strategy

13. Case: Hartford Steam Boiler Inspection and Insurance Company,
    9-675-088
    Reading: Skinner, "The Focused Factory," HBR reprint 74308

14. Case: Flair, Inc., 9-676-094
    Reading: Levitt, "The Industrialization of Service," HBR reprint
    76506

15. Lecture/Discussion
    Reading: Text, Chapter 5 and Appendix C

16. Case: Engineering Employment Exchange, Inc.*, 9-685-382
    Reading: Maister and Lovelock, "Managing Facilitator Services"

17. Case: American Home Shield Corporation*, 9-673-110
    Reading: Dearden, "Cost Accounting Comes to Service Industries,"
    HBR reprint 78503

18. Case: Rural Metro Fire Department, 9-681-082
    Reading: Packer, "Measuring the Intangible in Productivity"

19. Case: Federal Express (A), 9-577-042
    (TN: 5-577-189)

20. Case: Cunningham, Inc.: Industrial Service Group*, 9-581-022
    (TN: 5-585-066)

21. Case: People Express, 9-483-103 (Videos: 9-885-015, 9-885-016;
    TN: 5-486-004)
    Reading: Text, Chapter 7
    Reading: Berry, "The Employee as Customer"

22. Case: Smith Jones, 9-681-072 (TNs: 5-682-009, 5-682-016)
    Reading: Maister, "Balancing the Professional Service Firm"

23. Case: Mark Twain Bancshares, Inc.*, 9-385-178
    (Video: 9-886-006)

24. Lecture/Discussion: Review for Mid-Term Exam*

25. Mid-Term Examination*

Designing the Service Delivery System

26. Case: Medibus, Inc.*, 9-675-177
    Reading: Shostak, "Designing Services That Deliver"

27. Lecture/Discussion
    Reading: Text, Chapter 6

28. Cases: Buffalo Savings Bank (A) (with Buffalo Savings Bank (B)

to be distributed in class), 9-581-059, 9-581-060
(Video: 9-885-003; TN: 5-585-065)
Reading: Chase, "Where Does the Customer Fit in a Service
Organization?," HBR reprint 78601

29.   Case: North American Van Lines, 9-675-149 (TN: 5-677-114)
Reading: Sasser, "Match Supply and Demand in Service
Industries," HBR reprint 76608

30.   Case: Max Able Medical Clinic (AR), 9-676-179 (TNs: 5-677-100,
5-678-071)
Reading: Mills and Moberg, "Perspectives on the Technology of
Service Operations"

31.   Case: Francis, Berther & Allfreed*, 9-681-060 (TNs: 5-682-013,
5-682-009)
Reading: Hostage, "Quality Control in a Service Business," HBR
reprint 75405

Managing the Multisite Firm

32.   Case: Triangle Maintenance Corp., 9-572-030

33.   Cases: Dobbs House (A) (with Dobbs House (B) to be distributed
in class), 9-673-058, 9-673-059

34.   Case: Ryder System, Inc. (B)*, 9-573-043

Managing the Multibusiness Firm

35.   Lecture/Discussion
Reading: Text, Chapter 4

36.   Cases: Lyric Dinner Theater (A) (with Lyric Dinner Theater (B) to
be distributed in class), 9-386-056, 9-386-057
(Video: 9-886-023)

37.   Cases: CompuServe (A) (with CompuServe (A$_1$) to be distributed in
class), 9-386-067, 9-386-094 (TN: 5-386-086)

38.   Cases: Sears, Roebuck & Co. in the '80s (A)*, 9-386-029

Managing the Multinational Service Firm

39.   Lecture/Discussion
Reading: Text, Chapter 8

40.   Case: British Airways, 9-585-014

41.   Case: Benetton (A), 9-685-014 (Video: 9-886-010; TN: 5-686-019)

Conclusion and and Review

42. Case: Bradford Schools, 9-681-049 (TN: 5-681-075)
    Reading: Thomas, "Strategy is Different in Service Businesses,"
        HBR reprint 78411

43. Your School*

44. Lecture/Discussion
    Reading: Text, Chapter 9 and Concluding Remarks

45. Lecture/Discussion: Review for Final Examination*

**Management of Services: Five-Day Seminar, 9-200-102, and Three-Day
            Seminar, 9-200-103**

This course outline assumes four classes per day. Items marked with
asterisks can be eliminated for a three-day program or for a lighter work
load for a five-day program.

Day 1: The Strategic Service Vision

1. Case: Shouldice Hospital Limited, 9-683-068
    Reading: Text, Introduction, Chapter 1 and Appendices A and B

2. Lecture/Discussion
    Reading: Text, Chapter 2

3. Cases: Lex Service Group (A) and (B), 9-382-067, 9-382-068

4. Case: Benihana of Tokyo, 9-673-057 (TN: 5-677-037)
    Reading: Levitt, "The Industrialization of Service," HBR reprint
        76506

Day 2: Positioning the Service Business

5. Case: Southwest Airlines (A), 9-575-060 (Video: 9-883-010;
        TN: 5-575-134)

6. Lecture/Discussion
    Reading: Text, Chapter 3

7. Case: The Parker House (A)*, 9-580-151 (TN: 5-585-060)

8. Case: The Architects Collaborative, Inc.*, 9-575-016
        (TN: 5-810-070)
    Reading: Lovelock, "Why Marketing Management Needs to be
        Different for Services"*

Day 3: Developing the Operating Strategy

9. Case: Hartford Steam Boiler Inspection and Insurance Company*,

9-675-088
Reading: Skinner, "The Focused Factory"*, 9-675-088

10. Lecture/Discussion
Reading: Text, Chapter 5

11. Case: Federal Express (A), 9-577-042 (TN: 5-577-189)

12. Case: Smith Jones*, 9-681-072 (TNs: 5-682-009, 5-682-016)
Reading: Maister, "Balancing the Professional Service Firm"*

Day 4: Designing the Service Delivery System

13. Cases: Buffalo Savings Bank (A) (with Buffalo Savings Bank (B)
to be distributed in class), 9-581-059, 951-581-060
(Video: 9-885-003; TN: 5-585-065)

14. Lecture/Discussion
Reading: Text, Chapters 6 and 7

15. Case: Ryder System, Inc. (B), 9-573-043

16. Case: Triangle Maintenance Corp.*, 9-572-030
Reading: Hostage, "Quality Control in a Service Business,"* HBR
reprint 73405

Day 5: Concluding Topics

17. Cases: Dobbs House (A) (with Dobbs House (B) to be distributed
in class)*, 9-673-058, 9-673-059

18. Lecture/Discussion*
Reading: Text, Chapter 4*

19. Cases: Sears, Roebuck & Co. in the '80s (A)*, 9-386-029
Reading: McFarlan, "Information Technology Changes the Way You
Compete,"* HBR reprint 84308

20. Lecture/Discussion
Reading: Text, Chapter 9 and Concluding Remarks

**Services Marketing: Semester Course, 9-200-104, or Quarter Course,
9-200-105**

This set of assignments assumes a semester-length course of 45
sessions. Those specific items marked with an asterisk may be eliminated
to create a quarter-length course of 30 classes. The assignments purposely
have been designed to be ample. Those desiring to reduce the length of
each assignment might eliminate certain of the assigned readings outside
the text.

Introduction: The Strategic Service Vision

1. Lecture/Discussion
    Reading: Text, Introduction, Chapter 1 and Appendices A and B

2. Case: Benihana of Tokyo*, 5-673-057 (TN: 5-677-037)

3. Case: Shouldice Hospital Limited, 9-683-068
    Reading: Text, Chapter 2

4. Cases: Lex Service Group (A) and (B), 9-382-067, 9-382-068
    Reading: Lovelock, "Classifying Services to Gain Strategic
              Marketing Insight"

5. Case: Flair, Inc.*, 9-676-094
    Reading: Levitt, "The Industrialization of Service," HBR reprint
              76506

Positioning

6. Lecture/Discussion
    Reading: Text, Chapter 3

7. Case: L.L. Bean, Inc.: Corporate Strategy,* 9-581-159

8. Case: The Parker House (A), 9-580-151 (TN: 5-585-060)

9. Case: KCTS - Channel 9, Seattle*, 9-577-136 (TN: 5-578-063)

10. Case: The Architects Collaborative, Inc., 9-575-016
           (TN: 5-581-070)

11. Case: Health Systems, Inc.*, 9-580-115 (TN: 5-585-061)

Marketing Strategy: Advertising and Personal Selling

12. Lecture/Discussion
    Reading: Lovelock, "Why Marketing Management Needs to be
              Different for Services"

13. Case: Federal Express (A), 9-577-042 (TN: 5-577-189)
    Reading: George and Berry, "Guidelines for the Advertising of
              Services"

14. Case: AT&T Long Lines (A) Marketing Telemarketing*, 9-580-145
           (Video: 9-880-013; TN: 5-581-157)

15. Case: Cunningham, Inc.: Industrial Service Group, 9-581-022
           (TN: 5-585-066)

Marketing Strategy: Managing Demand and Supply

16. Lecture/Discussion
    Reading: Text, Chapter 5 and Appendix C

      Reading: Chase, "Where Does the Customer Fit in a Service
                    Organization?, HBR reprint 78601

17. Reading: Sasser, "Match Supply and Demand in Service
                    Industries," HBR reprint 76608

18. Case: Garber Travel Services, Inc., 9-677-210 (TN: 5-681-097)
      Reading: Lovelock and Young, "Look to Customers to Increase
                  Productivity", HBR reprint 79310

19. Case: American Repertory Theater*, 9-580-133 (TN: 5-585-062)

20. Case: Bridger Bowl, Inc. (A)

Marketing Strategy: Pricing

21. Case: Southwest Airlines (A), 9-575-060 (Video: 9-883-010)

22. Case: Marriott's Rancho Las Palmas Resort, 9-581-084
          (TN: 5-585-058)

23. Lecture/Discussion: Review for Mid-Term Exam*

24. Mid-Term Examination*

Marketing Strategy: Methods of Distribution

25. Lecture/Discussion
      Reading: Text, Chapter 6

26. Cases: Buffalo Savings Bank (A) (with Buffalo Savings Bank (B)
          to be distributed in class), 9-581-059, 9-581-060
          (Video: 9-885-003; TN: 5-585-065)

27. Case: Medibus, Inc., 9-675-177

28. Case: Supermarket Services, Inc. (SMS), 9-577-091

29. Case: Wendy's Old-Fashioned Hamburgers*, 9-677-122
          (TN: 5-677-220)

Quality and Cost Control

30. Lecture/Discussion
      Reading: Text, Chapter 7

31. Case: Francis, Berther & Allfreed, 9-681-060
          (TNs: 5-682-013, 5-682-009)
      Reading: Hostage, "Quality Control in a Service Business," HBR
               reprint 75405

32. Case: Triangle Maintenance Corp.*, 9-572-030

33. Case: People Express, 9-483-103 (Videos: 9-885-015, 9-885-016;
            TN: 5-486-004)
    Reading: Berry, "The Employee as Customer"

34. Case: Hewitt Associates*, 9-681-063 (TNs: 5-682-015, 5-682-009)
    Reading: Maister and Lovelock, "Managing Facilitator Services"*
    Reading: Dearden, "Cost Accounting Comes to Service
              Industries,"* HBR reprint 78503

Product Line Development

35. Lecture/Discussion
    Reading: Text, Chapter 4

36. Cases: Lyric Dinner Theater (A) (with Lyric Dinner Theater (B)
            to be distributed in class), 9-386-056, 9-386-057
            (Video: 9-886-023)

37. Case: Engineering Employment Exchange, Inc., 9-685-382

38. Case: Ryder System, Inc. (B)*, 9-573-043

39. Cases: CompuServe (A) (with CompuServe (A_1) to be distributed in
            class)*, 9-386-067, 9-386-094 (TN: 5-386-086)

40. Cases: Sears, Roebuck & Co. in the '80s (A)*,
            9-386-029

Multinational Marketing

41. Lecture/Discussion
    Reading: Text, Chapter 8

42. Case: British Airways, 9-585-014

43. Case: Benetton (A), 9-685-014 (Video: 9-886-010; TN: 5-686-019)

Conclusion: Services Marketing in the Future

44. Lecture/Discussion
    Reading: Text, Chapter 9 and Concluding Remarks
    Reading: Berry, "Services Marketing is Different"

45. Lecture/Discussion: Review for Final Examination

Services Marketing: Five-Day Seminar, 9-200-106, and Three-Day Seminar, 9-200-107

This course outline assumes four-class days.   Items marked with asterisks can be eliminated for a three-day program or for a lighter work load for a five-day program.

Day 1:   The Strategic Service Vision

1.   Case: Shouldice Hospital Limited, 9-683-068
     Reading: Text, Introduction and Chapter 1

2.   Lecture/Discussion
     Reading: Text, Chapter 2

3.   Case: The Architects Collaborative, Inc.*, 9-575-016
             (TN: 5-581-070)
     Reading: Text, Chapter 3

4.   Case: The Parker House (A), 9-580-151 (TN: 5-585-060)

Day 2:   Advertising, Selling, and Demand Management

5.   Case: Federal Express (A), 9-577-042 (TN: 5-577-189)
     Reading: George and Berry, "Guidelines for the Advertising of
                Services"

6.   Case: Cunningham, Inc.:   Industrial Service Group*, 9-581-022
             (TN: 5-585-066)

7.   Lecture/Discussion
     Reading: Lovelock, "Why Marketing Management Needs to be
                Different for Services"

8.   Case: Bridger Bowl, Inc. (A)*
     Reading: Sasser, "Match Supply and Demand in Service
                Industries," HBR reprint 76608

Day 3:   Pricing and Service Delivery System Design

9.   Case: Southwest Airlines (A), 9-575-060 (Video: 9-883-010;
             TN: 5-575-134)
     Reading: Text, Chapter 6

10.   Case: American Home Shield Corporation*, 9-673-110

11.   Lecture/Discussion*

12.   Cases: Buffalo Savings Bank (A) (with Buffalo Savings Bank (B)
               to be distributed during class), 9-581-059, 9-581-060
               (Video: 9-885-003; TN: 5-585-065)
      Reading: Chase, "Where Does the Customer Fit in a Service

Organization?," HBR reprint 78601

Day 4: Managing Product Quality and Offering

13. Case: Triangle Maintenance Corp., 9-572-030
     Reading: Hostage, "Quality Control in a Service Business," HBR
               reprint 75405

14. Case: People Express*, 9-483-103 (Videos: 9-885-015, 9-885-016;
            TN: 5-486-004)
     Reading: Berry, "The Customer as Employee"

15. Lecture/Discussion*
     Reading: Text, Chapter 7

16. Case: Ryder System, Inc. (B), 9-573-043
     Reading: Text, Chapter 4

Day 5: A Look to the Future

17. Case: Benetton (A), 9-685-014 (Video: 9-886-010; TN: 5-686-019)
     Reading: Text, Chapter 8

18. Case: British Airways, 9-585-014

19. Cases: Sears, Roebuck & Co. in the '80s (A)*,
             9-386-029

20. Lecture/Discussion
     Reading: Text, Chapter 9 and Concluding Comments

**Management of Service Operations: Semester Course, 9-200-108, or Quarter
                          Course, 9-200-109**

This set of assignments assumes a semester-length course of 45
sessions. Those specific items marked with an asterisk may be eliminated
to create a quarter-length course of 30 classes. The assignments purposely
have been designed to be ample. Those desiring to reduce the length of
each assignment might eliminate certain of the assigned readings outside
the text.

Introduction: The Strategic Service Vision

1. Lecture/Discussion
    Reading: Text, Introduction, Chapter 1 and Appendices A and B

2. Case: Benihana of Tokyo, 9-673-057 (TN: 5-677-037)
    Reading: Levitt, "The Industrialization of Service," HBR reprint
              76506

3. Case: Shouldice Hospital Limited, 9-683-068

Reading: Text, Chapter 2

Defining the Service Concept

4. Cases: Lex Service Group (A) and (B), 9-382-067, 382-068

5. Case: Garber Travel Services, Inc.*, 9-677-210 (TN: 5-681-097)
    Reading: Thomas, "Strategy is Different in Service Businesses,"
        HBR reprint 78411

6. Case: American Home Shield Corporation, 9-673-110

Positioning the Service Business

7. Case: The Parker House (A), 9-580-151 (TN: 5-585-060)

8. Lecture/Discussion
    Reading: Text, Chapter 3

9. Case: The Architects Collaborative, Inc., 9-575-016
        (TN: 5-581-070)

Developing the Operating Strategy

10. Case: Hartford Steam Boiler Inspection and Insurance Company,
        9-675-088
    Reading: Skinner, "The Focused Factory," HBR reprint 74308

11. Lecture/Discussion
    Reading: Text, Chapter 5 and Appendix C

12. Case: Engineering Employment Exchange, Inc.*, 9-685-372
    Reading: Maister and Lovelock, "Managing Facilitator Services"*

13. Case: Federal Express (A), 9-577-042 (TN: 5-577-189)
    Reading: Sasser, "Match Supply and Demand in Service
        Industries," HBR reprint 76608

14. Case: Hewitt Associates, 9-681-063 (TNs: 5-682-015, 5-682-009)

15. Case: People Express, 9-483-103 (Videos: 9-885-015, 9-885-016;
        TNs: 5-486-004)
    Reading: Text, Chapter 7
    Reading: Berry, "The Employee as Customer"

16. Case: Triangle Maintenance Corp., 9-572-030

17. Case: Francis, Berther & Allfreed*, 9-681-060
        (TNs: 5-682-013, 5-682-009)
    Reading: Hostage, "Quality Control in a Service Business," HBR
        reprint 75405

18. Case: Waffle House, Inc. (J)*, 9-672-101

19. Case: Smith Jones, 9-681-072 (TNs: 5-682-009, 5-682-016)
    Reading: Maister, "Balancing the Professional Service Firm"

20. Case: Mark Twain Bancshares, Inc.*, 9-385-178 (Video: 9-886-006)

21. Lecture/Discussion: Review for Mid-Term Examination*

22. Mid-Term Examination*

Designing the Service Delivery System

23. Case: Rural Metro Fire Department, 9-681-082
    Reading: Packer, "Measuring the Intangible in Productivity"

24. Lecture/Discussion
    Reading: Text, Chapter 6

25. Case: Medibus, Inc.*, 9-675-177
    Reading: Shostack, "Designing Services That Deliver"

26. Cases: Buffalo Savings Bank (A) (with Buffalo Savings Bank (B)
            to be distributed in class), 9-581-059, 9-581-060
            (Video: 9-885-003; TN: 5-585-065)
    Reading: Chase, "Where Does the Customer Fit in a Service
            Organization?," HBR reprint 78601

27. Case: North American Van Lines, 9-675-149 (TN: 5-677-114)

28. Case: Max Able Medical Clinic (AR)*, 9-676-179
            (TNs: 5-677-100, 5-678-071)
    Reading: Mills and Moberg, "Perspectives on the Technology of
            Service Operations"*

29. Case: University Health Service: Walk-In Clinic, 9-681-061
            (TN: 5-681-079)
    Reading: "Note on the Management of Queues", 9-680-053

30. Case: FBO, Inc., 9-678-117

31. Case: The Sea Pines Racquet Club*, 9-674-011 (TN: 5-677-038)
    Reading: Dearden, "Cost Accounting Comes to Service
    Industries,"* HBR reprint 78503

The Life Cycle of the Service Firm

Start-Up

32. Case: Safecard Services, 9-673-096

33. Lecture/Discussion
    Rapid Growth

34. Cases: CompuServe (A) (with CompuServe (A1) to be distributed in

class), 9-386-067, 9-386-094 (TN: 5-386-086)

Turn-Around

35. Cases: Dobbs House (A) (with Dobbs House (B) to be distributed
    in class), 9-673-058, 9-673-059

Multisite Operations

36. Case: Levinson Realty, Inc., 9-680-093

Multibusiness Operations

37. Cases: Lyric Dinner Theater (A) (with Lyric Dinner Theater (B)
    to be distributed in class), 9-386-056, 9-386-057
    (Video: 9-886-023)

38. Lecture/Discussion
    Reading: Text, Chapter 4

39. Case: Ryder System (B)*, 9-573-043

Multinational Operations

40. Case: Benetton (A), 9-685-014 (Video: 9-886-010; TN: 5-686-019)
    Reading: Text, Chapter 8

Summary and Conclusion

41. Case: Bradford Schools*, 9-681-049 (TN: 5-681-075)

42. Case: Your School*

43. Lecture/Discussion
    Reading: Text, Chapter 9 and Concluding Remarks
    Reading: McFarlan, "Information Technology Changes the Way You
    Compete," HBR reprint 84308

44. Lecture/Discussion: Summary of Course*

**Management of Service Operations: Five-Day Seminar, 9-200-110, and
Three-Day Seminar, 9-200-111**

This course outline assumes four classes per day. Items marked with
asterisks can be eliminated for a three-day program or for a lighter work
load for a five-day program.

Day 1: The Strategic Service Vision

1. Case: Benihana of Tokyo*, 9-673-057 (TN: 5-677-037)

2. Lecture/Discussion

Reading: Text, Introduction, Chapter 1 and Appendices A and B

3. Case: Shouldice Hospital Limited, 9-683-068
    Reading: Text, Chapter 2

4. Cases: Lex Service Group (A) and (B), 9-382-067, 9-382-068

Day 2: Positioning the Service Business

5. Case: The Parker House (A), 9-580-151 (TN: 5-585-060)

6. Lecture/Discussion
    Reading: Text, Chapter 3

7. Case: The Architects Collaborative, Inc.*, 9-575-016
           (TN: 5-581-070)

8. Cases: CompuServe (A) (with CompuServe (A$_1$) to be distributed in
            class), 9-386-067, 9-386-094 (TN: 5-386-086)

Day 3: Developing the Operating Strategy

9. Case: Hartford Steam Boiler Inspection and Insurance Company,
           9-675-088
    Reading: Skinner, "The Focused Factory," HBR reprint 74308

10. Lecture/Discussion
    Reading: Text, Chapter 5

11. Case: Federal Express (A), 9-577-042 (TN: 5-577-189)
    Reading: Sasser, "Match Supply and Demand in Service
              Industries," HBR reprint 76608

12. Case: Smith Jones*, 9-681-072 (TNs: 5-682-009, 5-682-016)

Day 4: Designing the Service Delivery System

13. Case: Rural Metro Fire Department, 9-681-082
    Reading: Shostack, "Designing Services That Deliver"

14. Lecture/Discussion
    Reading: Text, Chapter 6 and 7

15. Case: Buffalo Savings Bank (A) (with Buffalo Savings Bank (B) to
           be distributed in class)*, 9-581-059, 9-581-060
           (Video: 9-885-003; TN: 5-585-065)
    Reading: Chase, "Where Does the Customer Fit in a Service
              Organization?,"* HBR reprint 78601

16. Case: The Sea Pines Racquet Club*, 9-674-011 (TN: 5-677-038)
    Reading: Dearden, "Cost Accounting Comes to Service
              Industries,"* HBR reprint 78503

Day 5: Concluding Topics

17. Cases: Dobbs House (A) (with Dobbs House (B) to be distributed
            in class)*, 9-673-058, 9-673-059

18. Case: Ryder System, Inc. (B), 9-573-043

19. Lecture/Discussion*
    Reading: Text, Chapter 4*

20. Lecture/Discussion
    Reading: Text, Chapter 9 and Concluding Remarks
    Reading: McFarlan, "Information Technology Changes the Way You
              Compete," HBR reprint 84308

Three-Day Institutionally Oriented Seminars in Management of Services

Each of these course outlines assumes a schedule of three classes per
day.

Banking, 9-200-112

1. Case: Buffalo Savings Bank (A), 9-581-059
          (Video: 9-885-003; TN:: 5-585-065)

2. Case: Buffalo Savings Bank (B), 9-581-060 (Video: 9-885-003;
          TN: 5-585-065)
   Reading: Text, Introduction, Chapter 1, and Appendices A and B

3. Lecture/Discussion
   Reading: Text, Chapter 2

4. Case: Mark Twain Bancshares, Inc., 9-385-178 (Video: 9-886-006)

5. Lecture/Discussion
   Reading: Text, Chapter 3

6. Manufacturers Hanover Corporation - Worldwide Network, 9-185-018
   Reading: Text, Chapter 5 and Appendix C

7. Cases: Chemical Bank (A), 9-485-178, and (A) Supplement,
           A-9-172-288 (Video: 9-886-005)

8. Case: Chemical Bank (B), 9-485-029 (Video: 9-886-014)

9. Lecture/Discussion
   Reading: Text, Chapter 9 and Concluding Remarks

Communications, Information, and Media, 9-200-113

1. Case: Shouldice Hospital Limited, 9-683-068

2. Case: <u>The Saturday Evening Post</u>, 9-373-009

3. Lecture/Discussion
    Reading: Text, Introduction, Chapter 1, and Appendices A and B

4. Case: AT&T Long Lines (A) Marketing Telemarketing, 9-580-145
             (Video: 9-880-013; TN: 5-581-157)
    Reading: Text, Chapter 2

5. Case: CompuServe (A) and (with CompuServe (A₁) to be handed out
             near the end of class), 9-386-067, 9-386-094
             (TN: 5-386-086)

6. Lecture/Discussion
    Reading: Text, Chapter 3

7. Case: The Information Bank, 9-576-257

8. Case: Business Research Corporation (A). 4-285-089
    Reading: Text, Chapter 6

9. Lecture/Discussion
    Reading: Text, Chapter 9 and Concluding Remarks
    Reading: McFarlan, "Information Technology Changes the Way You
             Compete," HBR reprint 84308

Financial, 9-200-114

1. Case: Shouldice Hospital Limited, 9-683-068

2. Case: Progressive Corporation (A), 9-381-088

3. Lecture/Discussion
    Reading: Text, Introduction, Chapter 1, and Appendices A and B

4. Case: Mitchum, Jones and Templeton, Inc., 9-573-068
             (Video: 9-884-005)
    Reading: Text, Chapter 2

5. Cases: Sears, Roebuck & Co, in the '80s (A),
             9-386-029

6. Lecture/Discussion
    Reading: Text, Chapter 3

7. Case: Hartford Steam Boiler Inspection and Insurance Company,
             9-675-088
    Reading: Text, Chapter 5
    Reading: Skinner, "The Focused Factory," HBR reprint 74308

8. Case: VISA International: The Management of Change, 9-482-022
    Reading: Text, Chapter 7

9. Lecture/Discussion
    Reading: Text, Chapter 9 and Concluding Remarks
    Reading: McFarlan, "Information Technology Changes the Way You
              Compete," HBR reprint 84308

Food and Lodging, 9-200-115

1. Case: Benihana of Tokyo, 9-673-057 (TN: 5-677-037)

2. Case: Marriott's Rancho Las Palmas Resort, 9-581-084
           (TN: 5-585-058)
    Reading: Text, Introduction, Chapter 1, and Appendices A and B

3. Lecture/Discussion
    Reading: Text, Chapter 2

4. Case: The Parker House (A), 9-580-151 (TN: 5-585-060)
    Reading: Chapter 3

5. Case: Wendy's Old-Fashioned Hamburgers, 9-677-122
           (TN: 5-677-220)

6. Lecture/Discussion
    Reading: Text, Chapter 5 and Appendix C
    Reading: Levitt, "The Industrialization of Service," HBR reprint
              76506

7. Case: Waffle House (J), 9-672-101

8. Case: The Stanford Court (A), 9-680-009 (TN: 5-681-093;
           Video: 9-884-016)
    Reading: Hostage, "The Management of Quality," HBR reprint 75405

9. Lecture/Discussion
    Reading: Text, Chapter 7

Medical, 9-200-116

1. Case: Shouldice Hospital Limited, 9-683-068

2. Case: Health Systems, Inc., 9-580-115 (TN: 5-585-061)
    Reading: Text, Introduction, Chapter 1, and Appendices A and B

3. Lecture/Discussion
    Reading: Text, Chapter 2

4. Case: The Parker House (A), 9-580-151 (TN: 5-585-060)

5. Lecture/Discussion
    Reading: Text, Chapter 3
    Reading: Rice, Slack, and Garside, "Hospitals Can Learn Valuable
              Marketing Strategies from Hotels"

6. Case: Loma Vista Hospital
   Reading: Text, Chapter 5 and Appendix C

7. Case: Max Able Medical Clinic (AR), 9-676-179
          (TNs: 5-677-100, 5-678-071)
   Reading: Levitt, "The Industrialization of Service," HBR reprint
            76506

8. Case: University Health Service: Walk-In Clinic, 9-681-061
          (TN: 5-681-079)
   Reading: Maister, "The Management of Queues", 9-680-053

9. Lecture/Discussion
   Reading: Shostack, "How to Design a Service"

Professional, 9-200-117

1. Case: The Architects Collaborative, Inc., 9-575-016
          (TN: 5-581-070)

2. Case: Engineering Employment Exchange, Inc., 9-685-372
   Reading: Text, Introduction, Chapter 1, and Appendices A and B

3. Lecture/Discussion
   Reading: Text, Chapter 2

4. Lecture/Discussion
   Reading: Text, Chapter 3
   Reading: Maister and Lovelock, "Managing Facilitator Services"

5. Case: Law Offices of Lewin & Associates, 9-583-122

6. Case: Spanglett Associates, 9-681-080 (TN: 9-682-009)
   Reading: Text, Chapter 5 and Appendix C

7. Case: Smith Jones, 9-681-072 (TNs: 5-682-009, 5-682-016)

8. Case: Hewitt Associates, 9-681-063 (TNs: 5-682-015, 5-682-009)
   Reading: Maister, "Balancing the Professional Service Firm"

9. Lecture/Discussion
   Reading: Text, Chapter 7

Public, 9-200-118

1. Case: Shouldice Hospital Limited, 9-683-068

2. Case: The 911 Emergency Number in New York, 9-575-099
   Reading: Text, Introduction, Chapter 1, and Appendices A and B

3. Lecture/Discussion
   Reading: Text, Chapter 2

4. Case: Massachusetts State Lottery (A)
    Reading: Text, Chapter 3

5. Cases: United States Postal Service, 9-575-088
           (TN: 5-577-175)

6. Lecture/Discussion
    Reading: Text, Chapter 7

7. Case: Rural Metro Fire Department, 9-681-082

8. Lecture/Discussion
    Reading: Text, Chapter 5 and Appendix C

9. Lecture/Discussion
    Reading: Text, Chapter 9 and Concluding Remarks

Recreation and Arts, 9-200-119

1. Case: Benihana of Tokyo, 9-673-057 (TN: 5-677-037)
    Reading: Lovelock and Young, "Look to Consumers to Increase
    Productivity," HBR reprint 79310

2. Case: Bridger Bowl, Inc. (A)
    Reading: Text, Introduction, Chapter 1, and Appendices A and B

3. Lecture/Discussion
    Reading: Text, Chapter 2

4. Case: American Repertory Theatre, 9-580-133 (TN: 5-585-062)
    Reading: Text, Chapter 3

5. Lecture/Discussion
    Reading: Text, Chapter 5 and Appendix C

6. Case: Six Flags, Incorporated, 9-173-141
    Reading: Text, Chapter 6

7. Cases: Lyric Dinner Theater (A) (with Lyric Dinner Theater (B)
           to be handed out in class), 9-386-056, 9-386-057 (Video:
           9-886-023)

8. Case: The Sea Pines Racquet Club, 9-674-011 (TN: 5-677-038)
           Reading: Text, Chapter 7

9. Lecture/Discussion
    Reading: Text, Chapter 9 and Concluding Remarks

Trade (Retailing and Wholesaling), 9-200-120

1. Case: Carrefour S.A., 9-273-099

2. L.L. Bean, Inc.: Corporate Strategy, 9-581-159

Reading: Text, Introduction, Chapter 1, and Appendices A and B

3. Lecture/Discussion
    Reading: Text, Chapter 2

4. Case: Hills Department Stores, 9-577-024
    Reading: Text, Chapter 3

5. Case: Marks and Spencer, 9-375-358
    Reading: Skinner, "The Focused Factory," HBR reprint 74308

6. Lecture/Discussion
    Reading: Text, Chapter 5 and Appendix C

7. Cases: Sears, Roebuck & Co. in the '80s (A), 9-386-029
    Reading: Text, Chapter 7

8. Benetton (A), 9-685-014 (Video: 9-886-010; TN: 5-686-019)

9. Lecture/Discussion
    Reading: Text, Chapter 9 and Concluding Remarks
    Reading: McFarlan, "Information Technology Changes the Way You
              Compete," HBR reprint 84308

Transportation, 9-200-121

1. Case: Southwest Airlines (A), 9-575-060 (Video: 9-883-010;
           TN: 5-575-134)

2. Case: Federal Express (A), 9-577-042 (TN: 5-577-189)
    Reading: Text, Introduction, Chapter 1, and Appendices A and B

3. Lecture/Discussion
    Reading: Text, Chapter 2

4. Lecture/Discussion
    Reading: Text, Chapter 3

5. Case: Ryder System, Inc. (B), 9-573-043
    Reading: Text, Chapter 4

6. Case: North American Van Lines, 9-675-149 (TN: 5-677-114)

7. Case: Illinois Central Gulf Railroad, 9-583-083
    Reading: Text, Chapter 7

8. Case: People Express, 9-483-103 (Videos: 9-885-015, 9-885-016;
           TN: 5-486-004)
    Reading: Text, Chapter 5 and Appendix C

9. Lecture/Discussion
    Reading: Text, Chapter 9 and Concluding Remarks